SECOND COMMUNION

Bilingual Press/Editorial Bilingüe

Publisher
   Gary Francisco Keller

Executive Editor
   Karen S. Van Hooft

Associate Editors
   Adriana M. Brady
   Brian Ellis Cassity
   Amy K. Phillips
   Linda K. St. George

Address
   Bilingual Press
   Hispanic Research Center
   Arizona State University
   PO Box 875303
   Tempe, Arizona 85287-5303
   (480) 965-3867

SECOND COMMUNION

NASH CANDELARIA

Bilingual Press/Editorial Bilingüe
Tempe, Arizona

Library of Congress Cataloging-in-Publication Data

Candelaria, Nash.
    Second communion / Nash Candelaria.
        p. cm.

    ISBN 978-1-931010-56-6 (pbk. : alk. paper)
    1. Candelaria, Nash. 2. Mexican American authors—20th century—Biography. I. Title.

    PS3553.A4896Z46 2009
    813'.54—dc22
    [B]

                                  2008024707

PRINTED IN THE UNITED STATES OF AMERICA

Front cover: Photograph of the author at his First Communion

Cover and interior design by Bill Greaves

A few names have been changed to respect the privacy of the individuals mentioned.

Acknowledgments
Excerpts from this work appeared in a slightly different form in the following: *Homeground*, eds. Kathryn Trueblood and Linda Stovall (Before Columbus Foundation and Blue Heron Publishing, Inc., Hillsboro, OR, 1996); *Santa Monica Review*, Santa Monica College, Santa Monica, CA, Fall 2001; *Aztlán: A Journal of Chicano Studies*, UCLA Chicano Studies Research Center, Los Angeles, CA, Spring 2005.

For Doranne, David, and Alex

"Now, what's a Chicano?"

"If you've got enough money, you're Spanish," Tony said. "If you're poor, you're Mexican. If you've got the guts to raise your voice and protest, you're Chicano."

—Nash Candelaria
Leonor Park

CONTENTS

PREFACE

The dictionary definition of the word *memoir* gives the letter of what this volume attempts: a narrative composed from personal experience—an autobiography. However, such a definition omits the spirit, and it is the spirit that breathes flesh and blood into a life.

How accurately can any of us remember our lives forty or fifty years ago? Or last week, for that matter? Often in looking back we are not so much dealing with fact and accuracy as we are with impressions, feelings, partial knowledge, and half-truths.

In Akira Kurosawa's classic movie *Rashomon,* four people relate different versions of a violent incident in a Japanese forest. Each proclaims to be telling the truth. Lives outside of the movies are seldom so violent or outwardly eventful. Real lives are more like soap operas than Academy Award–winning motion pictures. Yet what truly happened is often beyond our ability to fully remember. The events of our lives are intensely colored by our histories, our prejudices, the unique filters of our personalities through which we view the world, and by our human limitations. Not to speak of the belief of some writers that the truth should never spoil a good story.

These memoirs consist of biased looks at selected events half-remembered, misremembered, misinterpreted, sometimes misunderstood—yet all were experienced with such emotion that they made a permanent imprint on me and still have great meaning decades later. The facts may not be totally accurate, but the feelings are.

The events related have to do with two questions: How did I become a writer, and what did I choose to write about? To me, writing means taking the chaos, the raw material, of every day and trying to give it order and meaning. It is a way to search for the truth, the *real* truth, facts aside.

Writing represents only a part—though an important and meaningful part—of my life. Like the four narrators in *Rashomon*, throughout my life I have selected and seen events through my own several filters: as writer, husband, father, son, brother, scientist, advertising professional, boss, neighbor, military officer, American, and member of a so-called minority. These are but a few examples of the many roles each of us inhabits in this rich, joyful, exasperating, all-too-short time we spend on this human plane—this time around. The first miracle is to have been born at all. Everything after can be a bonus.

These memoirs also have to do with how I discovered myself, my *true* self. Or at least the true self that I am at peace with, now that I am nearer to the end than to the beginning of my life. For in discovering myself I learned that I could not escape history even if I denied it. I could only create new history by how I chose to live.

We are all in a sense living history, carrying within us the marks of generations past whether we know it or not. We are history's success stories, for better or worse—the survivors—and we all leave the imprint of our lives, however faint, on the future.

Inscribed on the sandstone of El Morro National Monument, known as Inscription Rock, are the Spanish words "pasó por aquí," which mean "passed by here." El Morro was an important watering place for Spanish conquistadores and American travelers in the New Mexico desert during the sixteenth through nineteenth centuries—the New Mexico that is my ancestral home. The date alongside that inscription is April 1605. The name carved beside it on that cliff was Don Juan de Oñate, founder of the first Spanish settlement in New Mexico in 1598.

Just below, to the right of Oñate's inscription, is the name Joseph de la Candelaria. An ancestor, perhaps? Exactly who he was and when and why he passed through I will never know. But his name remains, the Spanish equivalent of "Kilroy was here." Another unknown traveler on his way through life. Another, like me, who pasó por aquí. Another faint imprint of history.

Inscriptions at El Morro National Monument in New Mexico.
The inscription on the left includes the words pasó por aquí *and the name*
Don Juan de Oñate. To the right appears the name Joseph de la Candelaria.

My eternal gratitude to publisher Gary Keller and executive editor Karen Van Hooft at the Bilingual Press for their support of my writing over these many years. My special thanks to Gary for conceiving the approach to this book, including the title, and to Karen and her staff for so wonderfully bringing that concept to fruition. Muchísimas gracias.

NASH CANDELARIA IN THE ROUND

What Goes Around, Comes Around

Nash Candelaria is one of our most enduring U.S. Hispanic writers. He is not only personally enduring; his oeuvre is inextricably tied to the struggle to sustain Hispanic culture in the face of countless adversities, and both he and his works cross two centuries. Nash started before the full advent of Chicanismo and Chicano literature, when he and others, such as Aristeo Brito, Ana Castillo, Rodolfo "Corky" Gonzales, and Miguel Méndez, had to self-publish for their work to see daylight. Then his historical novels won major awards and recognition, and his writing began to appear in what eventually has become too many anthologies to mention. His most recent works cascade into the postmillennial environment in which the Latino youth of California and elsewhere do not necessarily identify themselves as Chicano but as "mejicano," particularly if they are lowriding outside of the groves and ivory towers of academe.

In baseball there is a batting conceit that is known as the cycle, which is when a batter hits, in the course of one game, a single, a double, a triple, and a home run. There have been some pretty exciting cycles. A natural cycle, or making those hits in order, is quite a rarity. On June 3, 1932, Tony Lazzeri performed such a feat, completing it with a grand slam; in the same amazing game, Lou Gehrig hit four home runs.

And then there is the "hat trick," which in baseball slang is an obverse and converse cycle: one batter striking out three times in a single game. When a batter strikes out four times in one game, he has achieved a golden sombrero, and five in one game is considered a platinum sombrero. Six in one game? All things are possible in baseball and perhaps in New Mexican history as well.

It is longevity's rainbow. Six in one game is known as a Horn, after Sam Horn of the Baltimore Orioles, who performed it in an extra-inning game in 1991. Alexander Scott Gonzales of the Toronto Blue Jays tied the record in 1998.

Now, is it possible for a person to accomplish both a golden sombrero or better (better is used advisedly and ironically) *and* a natural cycle? Well, not in one game, but in one life? In the epic history of one people? If you sustain yourself long enough, you may just break on through to the other side.

Some of the highlights of the Nash Candelaria cycle include the successful self-publication of his novel *Memories of the Alhambra* (1977) under the colophon of Cibola Press and, beginning in 1982, his affiliation with the Bilingual Press/Editorial Bilingüe, marked by the publication of his second novel, *Not By the Sword*, and the Bilingual Press edition of *Memories of the Alhambra*. In 1991 he completed his tetralogy of historical novels, comprised of the aforementioned two as well as *Inheritance of Strangers* (1985) and *Leonor Park* (1991). In 2008 the Bilingual Press published his fifth novel, *A Daughter's a Daughter*, a powerful multigenerational work with a cycle of its own. The novel is about family loyalty, intrigue, and startling revelations and is set in a timeless but rapidly evolving New Mexico, where the first generation lived rural, confined lives, and contemporary manita women move into the mainstream and professional careers. The Nash Candelaria life-and-literary cycle includes the novels mentioned above, anthologies of short stories, major literary recognition (*Not by the Sword* received the 1983 American Book Award and was a finalist for the Western Writers of America's 1982 Best Western Historical Novel; "The Dancing School" was a finalist for the same organization's 1992 Best Short Fiction award; and *A Daughter's a Daughter* was a finalist for the 2009 Pen Southwest Book Award). And now we have the publication of his gripping memoir, *Second Communion*. Novels, collections of stories, a poignant memoir of considerable significance for understanding the twentieth century from a Latino perspective . . . when will it end? Hopefully, not soon!

Nash, born in Los Angeles on May 7, 1928, attended college at the University of California Los Angeles from 1944 to 1948, a time when the presence of U.S. Latino students in higher education was a rarity. His piece "Educated in Gringoland: UCLA 1944–1948" appeared in a special issue of *Aztlán, A Journal of Chicano Studies* (Vol. 30, No. 1, Spring 2005) that was dedicated to the University's relationship with its Latina/o attendees. From the title of Candelaria's essay, it is apparent that his presence at UCLA as a Hispanic student was unusual. Chapter 28 of *Second Communion* treats the same time frame and describes the author's experiences there in some depth.

The saying is "what goes around, comes around." On December 10, 1950, in Stockholm, William Faulkner gave his 1949 Nobel Prize for literature acceptance speech, which contained a well-remembered quote. The context for the quote is important. In 1949 President Harry S. Truman informed the American people that he had evidence that the Soviet Union had detonated an atomic bomb. On January 22, 1950, President Truman formalized a new cycle in the race for nuclear weapons.

> It is part of my responsibility as Commander in Chief of the Armed Forces to see to it that our country is able to defend itself against any possible aggressor. Accordingly, I have directed the Atomic Energy Commission to continue its work on all forms of atomic weapons, including the so-called hydrogen or superbomb. Like all other work in the field of atomic weapons, it is being and will be carried forward on a basis consistent with the overall objectives of our program for peace and security. (Harry S. Truman Library and Museum Web site)

Faulkner began his speech lamenting the deterioration of the human spirit.

> Our tragedy today is a general and universal physical fear so long sustained by now that we can even bear it. There are no longer problems of the spirit. There is only the question: When will I be blown up? Because of this, the young man or woman writing today has forgotten the problems of the human heart in conflict with itself which alone can make good writing because only that is worth writing about, worth the agony and the sweat. (William Faulkner Banquet Speech, Nobelprize.org)

Faulkner reminds us that humankind, and most especially the writer who is the species' oracle, must return to these problems of the spirit.

> He must learn them again. He must teach himself that the basest of all things is to be afraid; and, teaching himself that, forget it forever, leaving no room

in his workshop for anything but the old verities and truths of the heart, the old universal truths lacking which any story is ephemeral and doomed—love and honor and pity and pride and compassion and sacrifice. Until he does so, he labors under a curse. He writes not of love but of lust, of defeats in which nobody loses anything of value, of victories without hope and, worst of all, without pity or compassion. His griefs grieve on no universal bones, leaving no scars. He writes not of the heart but of the glands.

Then the Nobel laureate goes on to make these observations about prevailing rather than merely enduring, which ever since have remained a part of the Faulknerian canon:

Until he relearns these things, he will write as though he stood among and watched the end of man. I decline to accept the end of man. It is easy enough to say that man is immortal simply because he will endure: that when the last dingdong of doom has clanged and faded from the last worthless rock hanging tideless in the last red and dying evening, that even then there will still be one more sound: that of his puny inexhaustible voice, still talking. I refuse to accept this. I believe that man will not merely endure: he will prevail. He is immortal, not because he alone among creatures has an inexhaustible voice, but because he has a soul, a spirit capable of compassion and sacrifice and endurance. The poet's, the writer's, duty is to write about these things. It is his privilege to help man endure by lifting his heart, by reminding him of the courage and honor and hope and pride and compassion and pity and sacrifice which have been the glory of his past. The poet's voice need not merely be the record of man, it can be one of the props, the pillars to help him endure and prevail.

What, then, is new under the fifth sun/quinto sol? We are still afraid of being blown up. We still need to relearn the lessons of the spirit. We still need the writer's artistry to help us endure and aspire to prevail. And of course, all of this con safos with respect to the Chicano/Hispano testament. And we have Nash Candelaria to sustain us.

Candelaria tells us about pity and pride and compassion and sacrifice. He writes not of the glands, but of the heart. William Faulkner had Yoknapatawpha County. Gabriel García Márquez has Macondo, Rolando

Hinojosa has Belken County, and Nash Candelaria has the collective memories of the way we were.

In the introduction to a genealogy that Nash and his wife, Doranne, did in a manuscript intended for the extended Candelaria family, Nash writes:

> In a country where a person could become whatever his ambition, drive, hard work, and luck made of him or her, it did not seem to matter who his ancestors were. You were free to become more than they were, which was the goal of most who came here, shattering the shackles of the old social prisons of class or caste in the lands they left. One was too busy making his or her way to think about the past so that there was little opportunity to look back.

That is the conventional American posture. Even a successful candidate for presidential office ran with the emblematic campaign song "Don't Stop (thinking about tomorrow)". In the American way, it is the future that is important, not the past. And it's so easy to build up the future. It's always a day away. But that is not necessarily the Mexican American way. Nash has traced the Candelaria branch of his extended family to 1636. As you will learn in the following pages, the first known Candelarias to settle in New Mexico were Blas de la Candelaria and his wife, Ana de Sandoval y Manzanares. Blas died prior to 1680, the year of the Pueblo Revolt during which Spanish settlers were driven from New Mexico. In 1706, the Candelarias were one of the pioneer families that founded Albuquerque. That is a lot of history even by New Mexican standards; by American standards, it is beyond the pale.

One, Two . . . Many Communions

There are many ways to commune and a variety of objects that emanate a discreet charm for communality. Nash Candelaria's memoir runs from before his birth through his successful feat of self-publishing *Memories of the Alhambra*. That is a lot of Candelarian history, which at the same time parallels the span of New Mexican history, given the significance of the Candelaria clan for that region: first as perhaps one of Oñate's expedition who came to the region and left his marks on Inscription Rock; then as one of the pioneering families of colonial Nueva España; then of the northernmost reach (with southern Colorado) of alternating republics and empires of Mexico; then of a territory of the United States that became, on January 6, 1912, the forty-seventh state of the United States; and now of a postmillennial place that provides a glimpse of where our future is headed even as it is our region that is most rooted in tradition.

Nash and Doranne have provided this project with some poignant photographs that give added depth to the life of the Candelarias during the "early days." In some of those images, the twentieth and twenty-first century Candelarias are seen communing with, through historical traces, very early Candelarias indeed.

Memories . . . of the Way We Were

Someone (actually that "someone" is me, myself, and I) once jokingly told me that we macho victims suffer from Chicano/mejicano Alzheimer's: we only remember the grudges. It came back to me, crystalline, as one of a group of Arizona State University Hispanic Research Center researchers and cinematographers who documented the Museo Nacional de las Intervenciones of the Instituto Nacional de Antropología e Historia in Mexico City.

Wow, imagine that! A splendid museum entirely dedicated to the foreign invasions of Mexico! What other culture does something like this? Suddenly to be transported by magical museumology far from Lethe, Hades' river of forgetfulness, and returned whole in an exalted albeit nefarious condition. I felt much like Funes the Memorious, for whom only blind Borges or blind Homer could compose a suitable dithyramb for offensive and thus unforgettable memories.

The museum building itself is perfect. Originally the site of a teocalli dedicated to the god Huitzilopochtli in a village called Huitzilopocho (derived from *huitzilin*, "hummingbird," symbolizing the afterlife presence of Aztec warriors, and *opochtli*, "sinister" or "left-handed"), the Spaniards took it for their own and constructed what would be by 1676 a convent used as a school of theology and philosophy. Halfway through 1847 the Mexican military command, directing defensive operations in the central basin and facing the invasion of the United States Army, evicted the friars from the convent, which was partially fortified. On August 20th, as part of the "Heroic Defense of Churubusco," the corps of Independencia, Bravos, Victoria, Galeana, Tlapa, and the Compañías de San Patricio (Irish-American defectors from the U.S. Army who chose to fight on the Mexican side) defended the position before the main body of North American troops. In the end, the Americans took charge of the building, using it as an alternate prison with a small garrison. After the Mexican War it went through everything that Mexico went through: the Leyes de Reforma, the struggles of President Benito Juárez, service as a military hospital, and partial ruination by various contingents during the Mexican Revolution of 1910. In September 1918 Venustiano Carranza designated it as a museum, and in September 1981 it was transformed into what it is today: the museum dedicated to foreign interventions in Mexico.

The taxa are in place, supported by lithographs, flags, weapons, furniture, accessories both civilian and military, reproductions, and museographic recreations of events. They are all there, our grudges, nicely elaborated and adorned, in chronological order:

- Spanish Intervention of 1829
- French Intervention of 1838–1839
- North American Intervention of 1846–1848
- Second French Intervention of 1862–1867
- North American Intervention of 1915
- Punitive Expedition of the United States under Pershing in 1916

What does a traditional Hispanic litany of rancor over time immemorial have to do with Nash Candelaria's rendition of history as inextricably interwoven with personal destiny? Candelaria the contrarian.

Oh, there are plenty of defeats in his collective memory of the way we were. However, often enough they are handled—actually, "resolved" is a more apt word—with the elegance and parsimony of a people bent not only on enduring, but also on prevailing, no matter how dismal the circumstances. Coping with dilemmas that present themselves menacingly to his characters involves the deployment of the resources of the ancestral past. Interestingly, in a complex and stirring 2004 work of historical scholarship, *The Language of Blood: The Making of Spanish-American Identity in New Mexico, 1880s-1930s* (University of New Mexico Press), John M. Nieto-Phillips covers the same ground. Despite the vast differences in approach, both Nash's historical novels and Nieto-Phillips's works of scholarship complement each other. They both explore the relationship between historical circumstances and individual destiny. The personal and cultural issues are similar for both. Nieto-Phillips's preface contains passages that crisply elucidate the Candelaria novelistic and genealogical quest:

> As a child, I felt trapped by our supposed "Spanish" heritage. I was cursed with it. Double-bound by the pride I was supposed to possess and by the impossibility of speaking about "our history" among my friends, I grew ashamed of my family and our history. The source of that shame was the unspoken truth: that the grandeur of the past bore little relation to our humble, working-class status. . . .
>
> When my grandpa Tomás died, I was suddenly afflicted with a serious case of nostalgia. For reasons that have become only somewhat clearer to me with age, I yearned to revisit the dilemmas of my childhood, to recover that which I had repressed or forgotten—as well as that which never really existed. . . .
>
> This book is part of my migration back to New Mexico. It is my effort to come to terms with the contradictions of my family's lore that were the source of my shame and confusion as a young Chicano raised on tales of Spanish glory. (pp. xi–xii)

In his works, Nash Candelaria covers the biggies. The home runs (for one of the sides) and the triple plays. *Memories of the Alhambra* hones in on one of the great New Mexican predicaments: the resolution of the Hispano New Mexican identity out of the confluence of races and ethnicities, Spanish, Mexican, Amerindian, and of course, way out in right field, Anglo. *Not by the Sword* brings the gringo into the batting order in the cleanup spot, transporting us back to the years of the Mexican War with the United States (1846–1848) and evoking the historical and social circumstances that are suggested in *Memories of the Alhambra*. The opening lines of *Not by the Sword*, uttered by the protagonist José Antonio Rafa III, who is just home from his seminary in Mexico City, establish the struggle to discover heritage and identity: "Well, Grandfather. They say that we are to become Yankees now." Nevertheless, in the end, the novel is not so much about manitos versus gringos, but tradition and the continuing struggle to preserve it in the face of the American intervention that brings that tradition to the brink of collapse.

Inheritance of Strangers continues to chart the course of New Mexican-Anglo antagonism and rivalry in the forty years following the 1848 Treaty of

Guadalupe Hidalgo, the established event that created the Mexican American people (the Chicano period, according to Luis Leal, was not to emerge until the Sleepy Lagoon trials during World War II). Essentially, the novel is about the reappearance of organized Hispanic resistance against the domination of the smaller but more powerful Anglo elite. The Anglos have routinely bought Hispanic support for their elected candidates, but this time the campaign for election of sheriff leads to dissension within the Hispanic community, violence, and the formation of a vigilante group, los Hijos de la Libertad, in order to dissuade Benito Durán, the Anglo choice for puppet sheriff, from continuing his candidacy. The novel climaxes first with the death of one of the young Rafas and finally with the induction of another grandson, Carlos, into the ongoing saga and cycle of a manito community that initially endures and ultimately, outside the time frame of this novel, prevails.

Leonor Park, mostly set in Albuquerque during the Roaring Twenties, is a story of land and greed for land in a small town on its way to becoming a modern, twentieth-century Southwestern city. The protagonist, Magdalena Soto, has made an indelible impression on the reviewers of this novel as a character of outsized proportions.

The novel *Memories of the Alhambra* contains a key component that is subject to its own epic cycle. The novel opens with the death of the patriarch, José Rafa, a circumstance that causes his son, also José, to embark upon a quest for his beginnings, back to the conquistadores, the hidalgos (i.e., hijos de algo), and although the term is not used, the hideputas (sons of whores, i.e., illegitimates) as well, the fruit of the forced miscegenation between overlord conquistadores and conquered Amerindian women. José experiences a painful revelation when he journeys to Extremadura, birthplace of Hernán Cortés, and regards the bronze statue of the conqueror of Mexico. "If Cortés was your father . . . then your mother was—he did not want to think the next words. They popped out anyway. Malinche."

Malinche has been the whipping girl of a whole matrix of macho guajolotes for several centuries now. In Hispanic New Mexico, the term for turkey was for a long time the splendidly archaic "gainas de la tierra," but neo-Nahuatl or archaic castellano, as a Hispana Gertrude Stein might have observed, a turkey is still a *guaxolotl* is a turkey). The filósofos of the agravio never give a thought to the less-than-stellar performance of the male Amerindians in protecting their culture, preferring to blame women emblemized by Malintzin Tepenal for forced miscegenation. *Memories,* published in 1977, is written squarely in the "pinche, como duele ser Malinche" Chicana cultural frame of mind, but one that Chicanas were also using to carve out a place of comparative privilege for themselves in the new affirmative action–infused world of bicultural opportunity, particularly as related to dating mores in the novel environment of the groves of academe. For example, see the following excerpts from Chicana poems by Adaljiza Sosa Ridell and Lorenza Cavillo Schmidt in *Chicanas en la literatura y el arte* (El Grito book series, Year VII, Book 1, September 1973):

> Pinche, cómo duele ser Malinche.
> Pero sabes, ése,
> what keeps me from shattering
> into a million fragments?
> It's that sometimes,
> you are muy gringo, too.
>
> (Sosa Ridell, untitled, p. 76)

> A Chicano at Dartmouth?
> I was at Berkeley, where
> there were too few of us
> and even less of you.
> I'm not even sure
> that I really looked for you.
>
> I heard from many rucos
> that you
> would never make it.
> You would hold me back;
> From What?
> From what we are today?
> "Y QUE VIVA"
> Pinche, cómo duele ser Malinche.
>
> (Calvillo Schmidt, "Cómo duele," p. 61)

The revelation, the word that pops out anyway—Malinche—does José in. José dies of a heart attack on the bus ride from Extremadura (literally, "the land further out," or the "border land") to Sevilla. Poor, messed-up guy: he dies disappointed and unfulfilled in the knowledge that he is no pure-blooded Spaniard, but a member of the "raza cósmica," part Amerindian and part European. The novel doesn't end there. It begins with the patriarch, José Rafa, and then concentrates on the son, José, who, somewhat like Quentin Compson in Faulkner's *The Sound and the Fury* (signifying nothing), is broken by the "curse" of a past freighted with slavery and involuntary miscegenation. Yet, *Memories of the Alhambra* ends not with the death rattle of one who died consumed by the grudge held by "victims" of mejicano/Chicano Alzheimer's, but with the next generation, with Joe, José's anglicized son, who graduates from the university and marries an Anglo woman and who doesn't stop thinking about tomorrow.

The macho Chicano/mejicano remembrance of Malintzin Tenepal and malinchismo, fixed in the firmament of grudge, seething with hatred of the other and with self-hatred, is interesting, but it pales in contrast with the Chicana/mejicana confrontation of the "Malinche paradigm," as Sandra Messinger Cypess terms it in her valuable 1991 study, *La Malinche in Mexican Literature: From History to Myth* (Austin: University of Texas Press). In *A Daughter's a Daughter* (2008), Nash Candelaria takes us through this female existential gestalt as well. Contemporary Chicana/mejicana feminism makes mincemeat of macho meanderings about that Malinche, willing progenitor of hideputas. In her poem "La Malinche" in *Five Poets of Aztlán* (Binghamton, NY: Bilingual Press, 1985), Carmen Tafolla, for one, cultivates the image of Malintzin Tenepal as a brilliant survivor, a woman who made optimal use of her every intellectual, social, polyglottal, and carnal resource in order to rise from slavery to a position of great eminence in a cultural environment and historical moment of immense peril and utter confusion. And of course, grudges not withstanding, she was the first madre de la raza.

> For I was not traitor to myself—
>   I saw a dream
>   and I *reached* it.
>   *Another world* . . .
>   la raza.
>   la raaaaaaaa-zaaaaa . . .
>   (p. 195)

The last word on Malintzin Tenepal is surely not spoken. For one, the Tlaxcaltecas, erstwhile allies of the Spanish because of their implacable resistance to the sacrifice-thirsty Triple Alliance of Tenochtitlan, Texcoco, and Tlacopan, sometimes visually depicted her as the warrior closest to Hernán Cortés's side. Here is an image from the Lienzo Tlaxcala that copies images on the walls of the Tlaxcaltecas around the time of the war between the Triple Alliance and the Spanish and their allies from the city-states of Tlaxcala, Huexotzingo, Chalco, and others.

Tú, Sólo Tú

Because the memoir ends with Nash's triumph of writing and self-publishing *Memories* but refers summarily to the post-*Memories* fiction, with Nash's help we have selected some excerpts from his novels and one of his short stories that we believe provide an inkling of Nash's power and virtuosity as a writer and offer a splendid invitation to further explore Nash's literary body of work. The excerpts can be found on the Bilingual Press Web site at http://www.asu.edu/brp/Candelaria/excerpts.html. They include a sample of each of Candelaria's four historical novels as well as his short story "The Day that Cisco Kid Shot John Wayne" from the collection of the same name.

The excerpt from *Memories of the Alhambra* (pp 152–158) describes an interaction between New Mexican José Hernando Rafa and Señor Benatar, a Spaniard of Moorish descent whose family converted to Catholicism—although at first they furtively continued to practice Islam—to avoid expulsion from Spain. The conversation between the two evokes the cultural encounters that created what is now Spain and as a result provided a major component of the creation of Hispanic New Mexico.

The passage from *Not by the Sword* (pp. 72–80) treats a moment in the novel that reflects the presence, in 1846, preliminary to the Mexican War, of both the Mexican and U.S. armies, each on one side of the Rio Grande, in the area close to the Gulf of Mexico, near the city of Matamoros (literally, "Moor-slayer.") The selection from *Inheritance of Strangers* (pp. 9–14) introduces the reader to the lead character of the novel as an old man, in 1890, at Los Rafas, New Mexico.

"The Day the Cisco Kid Shot John Wayne," title story of the book *The Day the Cisco Kid Shot John Wayne and Other Stories* (pp. 7–22), introduces us to a milieu where kids of various racial, ethnic, and regional backgrounds interact with each other and with the silver screen, which in turn shows movies about such topics as conflicts between Anglos and Hispanics or American Indians.

The excerpt from *Leonor Park* (pp. 6–15) introduces us to Los Rafas, New Mexico, in 1985, at a moment when Antonio Rafa reads his son's play, "Nuestro Pueblo," set in the year 1912, which owes much to Thornton Wilder's *Our Town* but which has been rejected by the city's centennial committee.

A Daughter's a Daughter follows the Rafa family into the twenty-first century. In the excerpts (pp. 13–15 and 155–158), we see how the ancestral home in New Mexico becomes a backdrop as the changing roles of women in today's society in general impact the family in particular. As tradition reluctantly gives way to change, the circumstances of a new world begin to shatter time-honored mores and expose the secrets of a carefully guarded past.

It is with pride and pleasure that I give you *Second Communion*, Nash's memoir about how over the course of his life he broke on through to the other side and wrote and published *Memories of the Alhambra*. And the rest was history! Here is the record of the "early days" of an individual and of a community that not only endures, but despite its portentous challenges, prevails.

Gary Francisco Keller, Publisher
Bilingual Review Press

The Candelaria Family

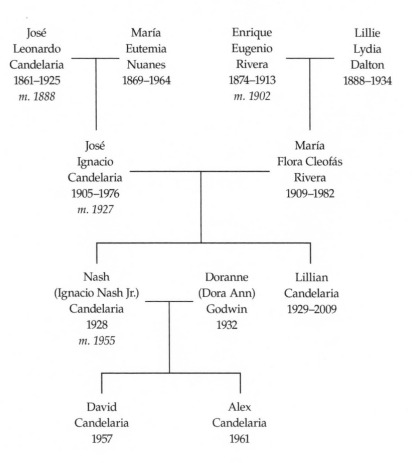

José Leonardo Candelaria 1861–1925 *m. 1888*

María Eutemia Nuanes 1869–1964

Enrique Eugenio Rivera 1874–1913 *m. 1902*

Lillie Lydia Dalton 1888–1934

José Ignacio Candelaria 1905–1976 *m. 1927*

María Flora Cleofás Rivera 1909–1982

Nash (Ignacio Nash Jr.) Candelaria 1928 *m. 1955*

Doranne (Dora Ann) Godwin 1932

Lillian Candelaria 1929–2009

David Candelaria 1957

Alex Candelaria 1961

ALSO BY NASH CANDELARIA

NOVELS
Memories of the Alhambra
Not by the Sword
Inheritance of Strangers
Leonor Park
A Daughter's a Daughter

SHORT STORY COLLECTIONS
The Day The Cisco Kid Shot John Wayne
Uncivil Rights and Other Stories

SECOND COMMUNION

1

In a way you could say that my family was one of the causes of the Los Angeles riots of 1992. Not the strong catalyst that the verdict in the Rodney King trial was. More like the first small grain of sand that started to irritate the oyster.

I had never thought of it that way until I received a folded message card from the hostess of a local radio program in Santa Fe, New Mexico, who planned to read from my writings. On the cover was the color reproduction of a detail from a mural titled "Labor Solidarity Has No Borders." The 25-by-48-foot mural, which is dedicated to the world's undocumented workers, is on the wall of the Southern California Library for Social Studies and Research in South Central Los Angeles, the scene of those riots.

On the back, just above a small reproduction of the entire mural, the card states: "The mural detail featured on this card is the green monster of imperialism, guarding the wealth of Los Angeles industry that has been created by labor. Also depicted in this magic-realist mural is a mass of working people cutting the electrified fence at the Mexican-U.S. border and worker figures with the faces of revolutionaries Malcolm X, Lenin, Marx, and Rosa Luxemburg."

But it was the message at the bottom of the card that really unlocked my memory. "These cards are available from the Southern California Library, 6120 South Vermont Ave., Los Angeles, CA 90044."

What was now the Southern California Library for Social Studies and Research was just three blocks north of the John Muir Branch Public Library, one of my meccas when growing up. The historic John Muir Branch of my youth had been closed for renovation in 1990. A temporary library, housed four blocks north, had been damaged by fire in the insurrection of April

3

1992. That old neighborhood was then serviced by a bookmobile in a vacant lot until the repaired temporary library was reopened in November 1993.

We had first moved to the then white, middle-class neighborhood in 1939, when I was eleven years old. Early in 1954, a few months after I had returned from service in the U.S. Air Force, my parents sold their frame house on West 59th Street to move to the suburbs of El Monte.

The grain of sand was that my parents had been the first in our immediate neighborhood to sell to a black family. Oh, the outrage and hysteria of some of our neighbors! The childless couple immediately next door, the business people who owned two dry cleaning establishments, were especially incensed.

"You just wait!" the man threatened my father. "I'm going to find out where your new house is and move the biggest, blackest, ugliest, trashiest family I can find right next to you."

Then, a neighbor woman and fellow Catholic, whom my mother had the good grace not to name, came by with her own injection of venom. "We should have known," the woman said. "When you moved into the neighborhood, we circulated a petition to keep out Mexicans. But we didn't get enough signatures."

My mother was stunned to learn this fifteen years after the fact. She didn't stay stunned long. She was a strong person, gentle and giving, but she didn't suffer idiots lightly. Anger took over—plus her strong belief that she could live anywhere she wanted and sell her house to whomever she pleased and to hell with you, madam!

My father seldom spoke of such things, and I don't recall that he did then. I had wondered what he truly felt, aside from wanting to sell. Because some years before, when I was in high school, he forbade me to bring my black friend to the house—of course, "Negro" was the term then in common use.

"What will the neighbors think?" he had said. What did I care what the neighbors thought? But it was my father's house, not mine, and powerless and frustrated as young people are in such situations, I saw my friend at school.

It was one of our many strong disagreements when I was growing up, including a later blowup over the ancestry of the girl who was my first serious romance. Her parents had been born in Mexico, and after all, we were New Mexico Spanish, descendants of conquistadors!

Flora

As for me, I could remember the excitement when my parents bought that house in 1939. My father was then thirty-four years old, my mother thirty—younger than my sons are now. It was a different world they lived in, having come to their majority during the Great Depression.

My father was the first of his family to leave New Mexico. He was raised on a farm on the outskirts of Albuquerque in a rural community named Los Candelarias, which his family had settled when the city was founded in 1706. My mother came from the urban barrio of Los Barelas, the poorest section of Albuquerque that was the way station for many displaced farm families who had lost or sold their land and were now trying to make their livings in the city.

It was the first house my parents had owned, and they felt very lucky to buy it—the fulfillment of the American dream. The down payment, though, had come hard: it was blood money. My father, who was a railway mail clerk, had been at work on board a Southern Pacific train that had crashed head-on with another train in the Imperial Valley of California. A brakeman had thrown a switch the wrong way. There was a long list of dead and a longer list of injured, including my father.

Because money was tighter than usual while father was in the hospital, we moved to a small apartment from the comfortable house that we rented on 58th Street between Figueroa and Broadway in Los Angeles. He had suffered a back injury, something that plagued him off and on for the rest of his life. It was the insurance settlement from the accident that became the down payment on my parents' first home.

This was the house that, looking back on my years growing up, I think of as home. It was the place where we lived the longest. Before, with my father's job on the trains and my parents' ambivalence about New Mexico versus California, we had moved back and forth many times.

But 1247 West 59th Street was home from the very beginning. Three blocks east, on Vermont Avenue, was John Muir Junior High School, which my sister and I attended. Along several blocks of Vermont Avenue was everything a neighborhood needed. There was the local movie theatre, purveyor of dreams during Saturday matinees. In the evening adults could see on the screen the swells in their fancy New York apartments wearing fabulous clothes, ready to go out and dine at the Ritz. On Bank Night, between features, the manager would come on stage and draw numbers while the audience prayed to fill

Ignacio

a row on their Keno cards so that they would win the coveted cash. "Come on, number 17! Baby needs a new pair of shoes!"

Down the block and across 58th Place was the Thrifty drugstore. Next-door was Kress's, where I bought my first tennis racket for fifty cents and indulged in Big Little books when I had the money. (Ten cents would buy you a fat little volume of the abridged *Tom Sawyer* or *Treasure Island* or, better yet, *Tarzan of the Apes* or *Buck Rogers*.)

On the corner of Vermont and Slauson Avenues was the local branch of the Bank of America. It was just across the street from Sears, Roebuck & Company where my sister, Lillian, worked part-time as a sales clerk as soon as she was old enough. And kitty-corner from Sears was the local food market where, during those tight-money times, you could buy a dozen small oranges for (if I remember correctly) one cent. Oranges that my mother would put in my brown paper lunch bag. When I ate them, they dripped and squirted their sticky, sweet juice on my hands and face, causing embarrassment in front of my school friends who had less messy matters to contend with in their lunch sacks.

Then north and south, a few blocks either way, were two other anchors of my growing up. South on 64th Street was the public library that, with the movies and radio, fed my thirsting imagination. North on 57th Street was Nativity Church, the Catholic residence of God, who stared hard into my wretched little soul, knowing exactly what kind of sinner I was.

What more could children want? Never mind that we were the only brown faces in our neighborhood and among the very few in our schools. The world was a wonderful place. People were friendly. We could never see behind the smiling faces of the very few who circulated petitions about Mexicans, who carried their bigotry hand in hand with their ignorance and their pained smiles. Nor could we imagine a neighbor's threats because we had sold our house to the wrong people.

As for brown faces, those were only seen in the mirror. Or when we visited cousins or family friends in the projects in the barrios of East L.A. or Boyle Heights. Or back where it all began, in New Mexico.

In benign memory, I couldn't imagine a better place to grow up. Marred only by the sweet pain of going back, years later, to see how it all had changed.

The year my parents sold that house had been the beginning of one of those great upheavals that permanently alter a city's landscape. The Harbor

Flora and Ignacio in Los Angeles

Freeway was coming through, eventually stretching from the shore at San Pedro Bay through central Los Angeles to the Civic Center and then north to Pasadena. All that was to remain of the house on 58th Street that my parents rented before my father was in that infamous train wreck was a massive concrete pillar helping hold up six lanes of fast, crowded, smog-belching freeway traffic.

The families displaced by this advancing juggernaut had to find elsewhere to live. In the early 1950s, this was west to those neighborhoods where people like my parents had preceded them. These first newcomers were black families. Then later, in the 1970s and 1980s, people came from Central and South America.

Years later, suffering an acute attack of nostalgia, I drove through that aging neighborhood. As I made my way along Vermont Avenue, up 59th Street past the junior high school and our old house to Normandie Avenue, and south toward Florence Avenue, I resolved that I would never go back again.

Most of the old stores were gone, replaced by others. Some of these had failed, leaving abandoned storefronts with broken windows and spray-painted graffiti. Across the windows of still functioning businesses were heavy black bars of iron grillwork. Off to the side of many entryways were folding-accordion metal grates, not quite as thick as the window grills. These would be drawn across storefronts at night and secured with heavy padlocks. And the movie theatre was gone! Where did neighborhood children go to indulge their dreams?

I don't think that the sense of dispiritedness was mine alone. It was more than the natural aging of a neighborhood that had been new in the 1920s. Poverty, that unwelcome plague, had infected it, bringing an aura of hopelessness that seemed to permeate the very air you breathed. It was no longer a memory of home; it was worse than those barrios in East L.A. where we visited poorer friends and relatives when I was a boy. It was a tinderbox waiting for a fatal spark. It was the American dream turned into a nightmare.

2

I first left New Mexico in the womb of an 18-year-old bride accompanied by her 22-year-old bridegroom on their combined honeymoon and move away from home. They were no doubt exhilarated, confused, frightened, and relieved at being able to bring forth this new life away from the prying eyes and shaking heads of family, friends, and neighbors. Five months later this love child shouted his first grito to the world in Los Angeles, a Californian by default rather than intent.

Forty-some years later, when I was participating in one of those New Age seminars that the Golden State was known for in the 1970s, the speaker turned to a large map of the United States mounted on the wall. "Show me home," she said.

There was no doubt in my mind. Without hesitation, I pointed to the state of New Mexico. The heart knows. There is something in our genes that is an emanation of our history. For I swear that a thin umbilical connects me back through the generations to those pioneer settlers whose inscription on Morro Rock simply reads "pasó por aquí." It connects me with pride in their courage and faith, in their toughness and tolerance, in spite of whatever cruelty and ignorance existed at the time. It connects me to what brought these strangers to this alien country long ago to help create this land of many cultures.

I am a true child of New Mexico's cultures: the Spanish whose surname I bear, the Native American whom many in the family will not admit to and whose looks and complexion I share, and a dollop of Anglo, like a latter-day grace note, to remind me that I am part of the mainstream, no matter what anyone else may surmise from my physical appearance.

But don't be misled. I was no stranger to my homeland. From my first grito to that seminar years later, there were many returns—most of them temporary. In the early years, these back-and-forth trips were more than the summer visits they would become later. For my father had passed a U.S. Civil Service examination and had chosen to become a railway mail clerk instead of a Border Patrol officer—candidates for both jobs took the same examination back then. Instead of life along the border of Mexico and the United States, there was that migrant movement to wherever shiny, parallel twin rails merged in the beckoning distance: El Paso when I was still a babe in arms; Albuquerque, where we lived for short periods; and finally, Los Angeles.

There are incidents from those first years that are remembered only because they were related as part of family lore, the stories that are told with amused smiles by parents and heard with embarrassed anger by small children. Such as when my little sister was born and I, a year and five months old and no longer the baby, shouted out in anger and hurt, "Take baby away!" Or there was the time when, at two years old, I had tried to drown the newborn kittens in the well. Then there is a photograph in the family album of a three-year-old boy in bib overalls, hair cut in Buster Brown bangs, captured by a Kodak box camera in mid-flight like a hummingbird momentarily at rest. It was taken, my mother said, when I had thrown a rock and hit her, proclaiming in Spanish, "Qué mona te puso," which means something like, "Boy, did I fix you!"

Then there's the kaleidoscope of things I actually remember from those very early years. Living on Roma Avenue in Albuquerque and going to an elementary school which no longer exists—was it Fourth Street School?—where the boys in first grade chased home a new student who did not speak their language. That student was me. The language I no longer spoke was Spanish. My vigilante pursuers, with little brown faces like my own, were intolerant of this . . . this . . . traitor, this villain, this stuck-up no-better-than-themselves who dared to be different. I recall my race home through the empty lot, preferring to run through the low-branched, stinging tamarisks that lacerated my face rather than submit to a beating from my pursuers. I arrived breathless and in tears, having learned one of my early lessons in intolerance.

Then, later still, there was the little stucco house on Fruit Avenue, since demolished to make way for urban renewal. I attended the third grade at St. Mary's Parochial School (which is still there). I had a hopeless crush on our

Nash at four in Albuquerque, NM

teacher, a beautiful, disciplinary nun, Sister Mary Margaret. Her face shone out of that starched white headdress covered by a wimple that was black like the austere, shapeless uniform that hid the rest of her—except for her pale hands and the polished black shoes that peeked from beneath the hem of her full black skirt—from worldly eyes.

Oh, I would have gladly suffered a martyr's death for Sister Mary Margaret. When she told me that rather than train to be an altar boy I should become part of the choir, I did not question her decision. Only years later, when I tried out for the high school glee club and failed, did it occur to me that carrying a tune was not one of my gifts. And the day that I went to school feeling ill, I fell asleep at my desk, awaking to the tittering of the class as Sister towered over me, had me stand and extend my hands, while she applied the Catholic equivalent of pep pills: three whacks with a wooden ruler. Even then I accepted the blame for falling asleep and did not fault her discipline. When, near the end of the school year, my father was transferred permanently to Los Angeles, I solemnly promised her that I would write. When I did, I fully expected a reply in perfect penmanship that would bestow some acknowledgment that I was special to her. But, alas, she never answered my letter.

At that same time, my headstrong younger sister had been enrolled in the all-girls' St. Vincent's Academy where, my father threatened, "The nuns will put some discipline into you." I'm not sure how well the nuns succeeded. What I do remember is that one day my sister's teacher asked the first-grade children, "What nationality are you?" What a question with which to confront the brown-faced girls whose parents probably spoke Spanish and who were no doubt confused about how to answer. There was no confusion in my sister's reply. "American!" she shouted with a six-year-old's authority. I never knew if that answer put an end to that bigoted nonsense. I hope so.

That was the last of living in New Mexico. From then on our home was Los Angeles, where I had been born. New Mexico receded in the challenge and excitement of a new school, a new church, and new friends. We did not live in those Chicano enclaves of East Los Angeles and Boyle Heights, although we had family friends and distant cousins who did. We were American, with every right to live wherever we pleased. In neighborhoods where children's parents worked at Ma Bell; or as sales people at the neighborhood Sears store;

or as house painters; or, as in the case of one man and his wife, who owned their own dry cleaning shops, the neighborhood capitalists; or as another entrepreneur who, born in Hungary, started out making a living from pennies dropped into the slots of peanut vending machines and worked his way up until he owned the restaurant franchise in a large department store. His garage was always loaded with goodies that I could sample because his two stepsons were among my best friends.

Lillian (front row, left) and Nash (front row, second from left)
at a birthday party

We were the only brown faces in the neighborhood and among the very few in school and church. My Catholic friends tended heavily toward Irish, with names like Blesser, Ennis, Fitzpatrick, Mannion, and O'Brien.

Then each summer we made our annual pilgrimage to Albuquerque, where, after about three days, my parents (especially my father) had the screaming meemies from the overattention and wrangling from relatives. This was especially true of my father's family, who insisted we visit with them first, stay with them first, and eat with them first. Damned if we did; damned if we didn't, like the baby claimed by two women before King Solomon. We were pulled in different directions until the least crazy-making move was to drive home, a decision that did not require the wisdom of Solomon. But in those few days, for all the turmoil, I wallowed in an embarrassment of family attention—from both parents' families.

The Candelaria family in Albuquerque.
From left to right: Flora, Nash, Ignacio, and Lillian.

3

The Candelarias and my mother's family, the Riveras, lived on opposite sides of town. Albuquerque was divided by Central Avenue (Highway 66), which ran east and west, and by First Street, which ran north and south alongside the railroad tracks, with First and Central being the center of town back then. The four sections of the city were defined with respect to this center. Los Candelarias was north of Central and west of First Street, thereby northwest. My mother's family lived south of Central and west of First Street.

In the earliest days that I remember, pre-World War II, Los Candelarias was country. The area was about four miles from downtown Albuquerque, far enough away to make the trip into town an adventure.

There were narrow dirt roads, including Candelaria Road, named after my family. The little adobe houses were separated by fields that still furnished a livelihood for many of the old-time farmers. At the junction of Candelaria and San Ysidro Roads was a small church, really a chapel, where a priest from Old Town Plaza's San Felipe de Neri Church came occasionally to celebrate Mass and hear confessions. There was also a small general store next door. A little over a mile west, Candelaria Road ended at the Rio Grande.

In contrast to the Candelarias, the Riveras were urban. My mother, Flora, was not born in Albuquerque. As a small child, she and her brothers and sisters had come with their mother from the village of Pecos in northern New Mexico. Like many poor country folk who for some reason had left the land, my grandmother Lillie had come to the city for work when, at age twenty-five, she had been left widowed with six children. My mother had been four years old at the time.

My maternal grandfather, Enrique Rivera, had delivered the rural mail on horseback between Pecos and Santa Fe. He had been a widower of twenty-eight when he married Lillie Lydia Dalton, a girl half his age. Her grandfather, Captain John Dalton, had come west with the army and settled in New Mexico. (Contrary to my youthful fantasies, we were not related to the infamous Dalton gang of the Old West.) Her father, Julian, had married a Sánchez and helped spawn a number of fair-skinned, Spanish-speaking Daltons. Some of them had blonde hair when they were young, making them conspicuous among their darker relatives at family gatherings.

As for grandfather Enrique, he had been quite a character, according to family lore. One of his favorite stunts was to ride his horse into the local dance hall and shoot out the lights. This unappreciated playfulness led to his early demise when an angered patron shot him in a barroom brawl. Dead at thirty-nine.

Grandmother Lillie eventually remarried a García and had another daughter, bringing the total number of children to seven. These maternal aunts and uncles, along with my seven paternal aunts and uncles—and their husbands, wives, and children—seemed like a cast of thousands to me when I was a child.

Summer visits to Albuquerque were rounds of calling on relatives, listening to the talk of old folks as if being let in on great adult secrets, and being entertained by country cousins who were tolerant of their city cousins' inability to speak much Spanish.

The beginning of all such visits was our dutiful call on my grandmother Eutemia Candelaria, known as Mina. Grandfather José Leonardo had died before I was born. Grandmother Mina had been blind for many years and lived to be ninety-four. She shared her little adobe house on Candelaria Road with my youngest uncle, Larry, and his wife and two small sons.

There was a small apple orchard west of the house, with gnarled little green fruit that gave you the collywobbles if you ate too many, a minor catastrophe when the only relief was a smelly outhouse barely within running distance of the house. Then behind and to the north, beyond the pump, beyond the woodpile, the chicken coop, the outhouse, and the main ditch, were fields that stretched to a neighbor's adobe house.

After visiting Mina came the visits to my father's siblings and their families. Aunt Conrada lived next door with Uncle Vincent Armijo, who had once been a professional boxer and who was then a short-order cook at the Coney Island in town, where chile dogs were a specialty. Then we would

José Leonardo Candelaria, 1861–1925

travel west along Candelaria Road toward the Rio Grande, turn right at San Ysidro Road—named after Isidore, patron saint of farmers—and go a half mile or so north, where a large plot of land stretched west from the dirt road over the acequia out toward the river. There, two of my father's sisters and his oldest brother lived on abutting properties with their respective families.

Uncle Gaspar, named after one of the wise men who followed the star to Bethlehem, lived on the front plot of land. His large adobe house stood high off the ground with a sloped roof, American style, towering over the flat-roofed adobes sprinkled across the landscape. He built the house himself many years ago, he once told me proudly, and it was as sturdy as ever.

Uncle Gaspar and his wife, Aunt Olojia, who we called Aunt Coca, lived childless in adobe splendor. Their eleven nieces and nephews from the flat-roofed, smaller adobe houses beyond the acequia more than made up for their lack of children.

Aunt Plajeres, mother of five of those cousins, was married to Uncle Florencio Perea, who at one time was a gardener at the University of New Mexico. Across a finger of cornfield lived Aunt Tocha with six children and their father, my Uncle Estaquio Gallegos. Uncle Estaquio was a handsome man who was heavily involved in local politics. His left wrist ended in a stump, the result of an accident in the sawmill where he had worked.

The last of the Candelaria aunts, Predicanda, did not live in the farming area of Los Candelarias like the others. To visit her and Uncle Joe in Los Griegos, you continued north on San Ysidro Road to Griegos Road and went east a bit to the American-style sloped-roof adobe where they lived with their one off-spring, my cousin Pete. Aunt Predi was the oldest of my grandmother's eight children. She always seemed calmer, more settled, and less high-strung than her younger sisters. Part of that may have been because her husband, José María Griego, was himself a calm and gentle man who worked for the local dairy.

The second oldest of the Candelaria uncles, Liberato, did not live in the country at all. He was the pioneer, leading the way from the farm into the wider world. He was a carpenter, a contractor, a builder—not only of houses but also of bridges to what Chicanos now refer to as the mainstream. With his wife and three children, all of whom graduated from the University of New Mexico, he lived on New York Avenue just north of the country club. Even the name of the street on which he lived reflected his outward thrust. It was not *Candelaria* Road, nor *San Ysidro* Road, nor *Griegos* Road. It was New York Avenue.

Nash's grandmother Eutemia (far left) as a young woman in 1894.
Seated on her lap is daughter Predicanda, and the little boy next to her is son Gaspar.

It was this brother, I intuited, who encouraged my father to move from the farm to the greater world. Or perhaps this was not intuition at all, but a construct of my fantasies about the past, fed by letters written from France and Germany when my uncle was a doughboy during World War I. Letters to his young teenage brother, my father, who was home helping to tend the chickens and the cornfields while big brother was off fighting the Huns.

The visits to my mother's family are less clear. Perhaps because my Grandmother Lillie died at age forty-six, when I was but six years old, while Grandmother Eutemia lived thirty years longer. Then too, some of my mother's siblings were younger and more like older cousins than aunts or uncles.

My Aunt Agnes and Uncle Cipriano were the youngest, not yet old enough to marry, and living with one or the other of their relatives after my grandmother died. My Uncle Albert, a lifelong bachelor, had moved to Los Angeles where he worked for the post office. Uncle Henry had not married until he came back from World War II, so his children were much younger than my sister and I.

This left the families of my mother's older sisters, Jenny and Rose. Jenny's first child, Reina, was deaf. Aunt Jenny's son, Robert, the child from a second marriage, was too young for us to know when growing up.

So it was that the cousins we saw most were the children of our Aunt Rose: Ben and twins Mary Ann and Mary Lou. All were fair skinned, and in childhood Ben and Mary Ann had blonde hair like their mother, a wonder among our other dark-haired, dark-complected cousins. Their father, Uncle Herminio Chávez, had been on the local radio as a musician in the early days. Later he became active in local politics, eventually being elected a justice of the peace. He then decided to run for sheriff, against the wishes of the local politicos. After a political rally he was found brutally beaten in an alley. He retired from politics after leaving the hospital and opened a general store that he and Aunt Rose operated.

Here, then, was the second of the two worlds in which I grew up. There was Los Angeles and mainstream middle America where we were different and in the minority, making our way in the Anglo world. And there was New Mexico where family and friends were warm, receptive, and definitely like us. We faced difficult questions: Could we belong to both worlds, or must we, like others we knew, belong to only one? If so, which one? Or would we be like those rare tortured and alienated souls who belong to neither?

4

Hispanic New Mexicans, the old-timers, take great pride in their Spanish heritage. The first colonization was in 1598. (The Pilgrims landed at Plymouth Rock in 1620.) The state capitol, Santa Fe, dates back to 1610, the oldest capitol and the second oldest city in what is now the United States of North America. Only St. Augustine, Florida, founded in 1565 by the Spanish, is older.

New Mexico existed as a Spanish colony until 1821, when New Spain (Mexico) along with other colonies in Latin America threw off the Spanish yoke. From that time on New Mexico was the northernmost province of the country of Mexico until the American conquest of 1846.

As Don José Rafa, a character in my novel *Not by the Sword*, says to his grandson when told that the Yankees are coming:

> "What does it matter, Yankees? I was born over ninety years ago on this rancho, praise be to God. Born a citizen of the Spanish Empire in this miserable, God-forsaken kingdom of New Mexico. I have never been to Spain. I will never see it. I assume that it is much like this. With people like us—except for the Indians.
>
> "And you. Look at you. Born on this same rancho twenty-five years ago, which makes you a Mexican. My own grandson born a Mexican.
>
> "And now. If a great-grandchild of mine is born on this same rancho next year, you tell me he'll be a little Yankee? Bah! We have always been here, and the world keeps changing. It's lunacy. The Yankees are coming. Who cares? What difference does it make? It doesn't matter."

But, of course, it did matter. Yet through the social and political upheavals old-time New Mexicans have maintained their Spanish claims. No matter that there have been intermarriages with Native Americans and later with those of European ancestry other than Spanish. There is pride in having survived centuries of hardship in a hard country, conflicts with Native Americans, and military and cultural conquest by Americans.

The pioneers who came west by covered wagon after 1846 faced many dangers, often to arrive in towns like Santa Fe that had existed for two hundred and fifty years. This is not to demean the courage and hardiness of these early American pioneers. But I can never look at a western movie—filled with modern American myth and bullshit—without a feeling of irony and a sense of disappointment. Where are the New Mexicans and those then-peaceful Pueblo tribes who lived with them, side by side?

There is a regular column in *New Mexico Magazine*, published by the State Department of Tourism, called "One of Our 50 Is Missing." Each month letters mailed in by readers cite the ignorance of outlanders. Queries like "Do I need a passport to go to New Mexico?" "How much postage does it take to mail a letter to that foreign city, Albuquerque?" "Is a special permit required to drive my car over the border?" "Will I need an interpreter when I get to Santa Fe?"

The column provides chuckles and an opportunity for indignation by local folks who know better. But it can also be read as a metaphor for the state and especially for New Mexico Hispanics. I have never heard of such questions by people going to New Hampshire or New York. No one mistakes them for parts of England. Or questions about New Jersey such as "Do the cows bite?" But New Mexico! Somehow, to many, it and its Hispanic people are foreign; never mind that they have been Americans for generations.

Therefore when my two sons were growing up, I wanted them to know more about their New Mexico heritage. And here in the United States, where few know their ancestry beyond their grandparents or some assumptions about their surnames, Spanish and Mexican archives and Catholic Church records go back to the early settlement of New Mexico. These threads connect us to the past and no doubt contribute to our pride of heritage. You cannot be proud of what you do not know. It's hard to know where you are going with your life if you don't know where you come from.

One major and invaluable contribution to this self-knowledge was the book *Origins of New Mexico Families: A Genealogy of the Spanish Colonial Period* by Fray Angélico Chávez, a Franciscan priest and descendant of an old New Mexico family. First published in 1954 and revised in 1992, it was a by-product of years of research on the Franciscan Missions of New Mexico and on the religious statue La Conquistadora, which is venerated by Catholic New Mexicans and resides in the Santa Fe cathedral.

It was here I began this quixotic journey to discover the past. An entry in "Part One: The Seventeenth Century" in Chávez's book reads as follows:

CANDELARIA

Blas de la Candelaria does not appear in any records of the 1680 Indian Rebellion or those prior to it. But among the native New Mexicans in dire need at Corpus Christi de Ysleta in 1684 appears "the widow of Blas de la Candelaria." She was Ana de Sandoval y Manzanares, who returned with her children after the Reconquest. This shows that Blas had died before 1680 and that his sons were minors at that time and, therefore, were not listed among the exiled colonists.

The Candelarias were survivors of the Pueblo Revolt of 1680, when Native Americans drove the Spanish from the settlements that stretched from Taos in the north to what is now Ciudad Juárez in Mexico. In their rage at years of oppression, Pueblo warriors killed missionaries and families, took women and children prisoners, desecrated churches, and destroyed settlements.

With other families, Widow Candelaria and her children lived in exile in what is now part of El Paso, Texas, until the reconquest and resettlement that took place from 1692 to 1693, when the settlers, led by Don Diego de Vargas, returned to peaceful pueblos and to what remained of the homes they had left. Two of Widow Candelaria's sons, Feliciano (Félix) and Francisco, later were among the founding families of the Villa de Albuquerque in 1706. According to records, they were both probably thirty-eight years of age (were they twins?), married, and had children of their own.

It was in Los Candelarias, a small farming community north of Albuquerque, where my father, José Ignacio, was born in 1905. As was his father before him, José Leonardo, the twin of Antonio Ignacio.

How does one search for any connection between José Leonardo and either Feliciano or Francisco? There were two prime sources: the Coronado Special Collections Library of the Zimmerman Library at the University of New Mexico in Albuquerque and the New Mexico State Records Center and Archives in Santa Fe.

Aside from the mystery of family connections to the past, there was another matter of intense curiosity to a writer. Francisco's son Juan Antonio dictated reminiscences that were an early (and somewhat faulty) history of New Mexico. This was in 1776 or 1777 when he was more than eighty years of age. Juan Antonio might have been better described as a fiction writer than a historian, and perhaps it was from him that I inherited my inclinations.

But genealogical detective work can be confusing. Baptismal records of the Villa de Albuquerque were missing for the years 1727 through 1742 and 1803 through 1821. Recorded baptismal records may have been incomplete or dates misrecorded. More than one person may have been born about the same time with the same name. The same person may be recorded by different names in different documents. Men frequently remarried when wives died in childbirth. Surnames often had several spellings—my paternal grandmother's maiden name appeared in three variations: Nuanes, Nuanez, and Noanes.

A combination of baptismal records, marriage records, and colonial censuses led this branch of the Candelaria family back to Miguel, husband of Marta Perea, married on June 16, 1744. Birth records were not found for either of them, but they were likely born some fifteen to twenty-five years before they married. A dead end. This left an unsolvable gap, but it is probable that Miguel was a grandson of either Feliciano or Francisco.

One of the amazing findings in this unsuccessful search was something unexpected. It was the proliferation of names as one goes back, the incredible web of connections. In the incomplete information for just these few generations there were Candelaria, Rivera, Nuanes, Dalton, Armijo, Gutiérrez, Sánchez, Gonsales, Sisneros, Martines, Durán, and Perea, all direct line ancestors.

It was a mind-blowing recognition. This surname with which we are tagged at birth and to which we claim identity, is but the tip of the iceberg. From the present back to those first Candelarias known in New Mexico represents ten generations. Standing here now, if I add up all my progenitors, each of whom had two parents, the total would come to more than a thousand people. I could hire a big hall and hold a convention!

Can you imagine a family reunion of ten generations of your ancestors? If you have trouble getting along with some of your relatives now, think about ten generations of them! Their clothes would differ, their levels of education and literacy, the social assumptions on which they base their lives. The way language changes, you might not even be able to communicate with them easily. The black sheep might be there, with rope burns around his neck from when he was suspended from the nearest tree. The family gossip would be pointing out exactly which tree he hung from. And somewhere in that crowd might be your twin, that other you who lived at another time, raising serious doubts about your uniqueness, not to mention your disbelief in reincarnation.

All this gave me pause about tracing my ancestral roots. First of all, it is sheer accident that I'm known by the surname Candelaria. In a matrilineal society I would have been known as Rivera. The shortsightedness of being tagged forever by that one name completely blinded me to all the other names that are equal parts of my history. It narrowed my focus, contributed to that common (some claim natural) tendency toward xenophobia that seems more a product of ignorance than reality. In a sense, I am a brother to many—not just in spirit and attitude, but also in blood. I must be related to half the people in the state of New Mexico! For all the real meaning in the surname Candelaria, I might as well have a barcode stamped on my forehead that says ABCXYZ or 101101. The name is just a convenient handle, a means of identification as well as a tool by which we can trace the connections that, like a spiderweb, connect to family, clan, and tribe.

The other issue it raises, of course, is does it matter? In the ultimate ideal world, of course it wouldn't. In this imperfect human world, the answer is not so simple. Yet, all I could think in looking back was, "That's nice. My sons might find it interesting." But history is over and done with. It can't be changed. What's important is to learn something from it. Where do you go from here? How do you become who and what you want to be? How did this Candelaria become a writer?

5

If I had been born fair haired and fair skinned with the surname Dalton, how different might my life have been? Why is it that only certain people get asked about their names? People named Dalton aren't. But this person named Candelaria definitely has been. "What kind of a name is that?" I heard over and over in my youth. "Spanish," I would say, not without a sense of awkwardness and embarrassment.

Why would anyone ask that? Was it so rare? I remember my father once proclaiming, not without pride, that we were the only Candelarias in the Los Angeles telephone directory. Rare meant valuable—if you were a jewel or a painting. But what if you're only a boy? Then rare meant different, strange. My father's observation did not satisfy me. The other Candelarias were probably too poor to have telephones, I countered.

There may even have been a few who heard me answer Spanish, and smiled. *Spanish* was polite for *Mexican,* and since I spoke without accent, like everyone else, maybe *Spanish* was correct. They weren't going to raise the issue.

But the issue was raised at home by not being mentioned at all. Mexicanness was not something we talked about. "We are," my father said, "Spanish! Descendants of conquerors!"

I would look at him, at his dark face with a hint of the Pueblos. I would look at myself in the mirror, my father's son, and wonder. My uncertainty was reinforced some years later when I needed a copy of my birth certificate for some reason or other and found I had two: an original and a revised version.

Whereas on the original the name of the child was given as Baby Candelaria, the revised stated Nash Candelaria Junior. On the revised certificate in the section for corrections to the original it stated: "Age of father, race of father and mother, occupation of father." Father's age was corrected

Ignacio, February 1927

from twenty-two to twenty-three. Color or race of father and mother were changed from Mexican to white Spanish American for father and white Spanish-Anglo American for mother. Father's occupation was changed from laborer to unemployed schoolteacher. The original was dated May 7, 1928; the revised certificate was dated April 22, 1942. My young parents were too timid to speak out, I thought. They were identified incorrectly by medical (and societal) preconceptions of the time.

About the time that I encountered my birth certificates I became aware of something else. I did know that my father suffered from stomach ulcers. He would go on his periodic diets of baby food and milk, avoiding the spicy chile that is part of any New Mexican's diet. What I didn't know until then, finally learning from a combination of parents' conversations and overhearing relatives in New Mexico, was that ulcers were not the exclusive property of my father. All three of his brothers and all four of his sisters suffered from the same malady as adults.

I ascribed it to temperament. Some of the Candelarias were pretty volatile and emotional people. Only later did I wonder what part stress played in their being born on the Spanish-speaking farm, and then being thrust into the competitive Anglo general society—a world they never made. I can remember one comment that my father received from his doctor: "It's not what you eat. It's what's eating *you*."

Then, years later, after my father died and my first novel was published (a novel about Mexicanness), my mother said cryptically, "You don't know how hard it was on your father, what he had to put up with."

She never explained beyond those few words. I had to use my imagination. He was one of the first Spanish-surname New Mexicans to enter the U.S. Postal Service. A typical shift of work might be two days and a night, traveling on the train from Los Angeles to Tucson, Arizona, and back. There would be the need for a hotel room in Tucson to sleep before taking the train back to Los Angeles. He would have to eat in restaurants.

Who knows what kind of so-called good-natured ribbing there might have been from fellow workers? Ethnic jokes about Pedro and Pancho, Speedy González. Not to mention signs posted in cafes as there were in the West in those days (or even now): "No Mexicans or dogs allowed."

These were things, my mother implied, that I would never have to deal with. And I saw this game of self-identification as Spanish as something

Nash circa 1928

more. More than self-deception. More than self-loathing. More than allowing society to impose its definition on you. It was an attempt at survival.

I also saw it, I realized, during the Watts riots in 1965. I was living in ultra–right wing Orange County, California. It was a year after my wife and I had worked with local church groups for fair housing in the county, an effort that was soundly defeated at the polls two to one. It was the same year that Barry Goldwater was nominated as the Republican Party's presidential candidate and that Orange County John Birch Society members and their fellow travelers thought that the millennium had come.

At the time I was commuting to my job as an account executive in an advertising agency on posh Wilshire Boulevard in Los Angeles. I had driven along the Santa Ana Freeway, crossed the Harbor Freeway, and was on the Santa Monica Freeway heading west. Traffic came to a standstill. I exited the freeway, driving along narrow side streets and finally headed north along Vermont Avenue toward Wilshire Boulevard.

On this particular day there was smoke clouding the air south and east of my destination. The police and National Guard were still trying to restore order in that part of the city.

Street traffic was light. The sidewalks were almost empty. Fear stalked the city.

Suddenly, up ahead on the left, I saw a gangling figure, hatless in khaki military fatigues that had seen better days. He looked like a marionette walking in a spastic almost-dance as if controlled by invisible strings. When I drove alongside, I looked over. He looked back at me. It was a young black man, fear evident on his face as he walked in this white part of town. He made a feeble attempt at a smile, leaned slightly toward me, waved a hand, and shouted. The car window was closed. I couldn't hear. But the shape of his mouth formed the words, "Friends! We're friends!"

I thought of my father. "Spanish. We're Spanish."

I was overcome with sadness that anyone had to go through life in fear and abasement because of their color. I nodded and waved at the young man in his khaki costume, his outward sign of belonging that beseeched acceptance. Then I drove on toward Wilshire Boulevard, crowded with people who had never been to Watts and would probably never have heard of it except for the riots.

6

Unbeknownst to me, the first signs of the budding writer manifested themselves at John Muir Junior High School. My schooling there started in 1938, the year before my parents bought the house on 59th Street. My father had been in the hospital. We were living in a small apartment about a mile from school, so naturally I walked.

This was the time when there were no such things as gifted programs. Forty students per class was the norm. And having survived the gauntlet of parochial school, public school seemed easy. I accepted it as a matter of course that I should skip grades, so that by junior high I was two years ahead of my age group. Academically I was advanced; socially, still a little kid. I was also the smallest boy in class.

At John Muir Junior High School, I think I was taught all the English grammar that I ever learned. Two drillmasters still live in my memory: Mr. Toomey and Mrs. Heidergutt (you can imagine the fun junior high boys had with her name).

Mr. Toomey took over this raw clay of a classroom in seventh grade. The boys had unkempt hair and aromatic tennis shoes. They smelled and acted like puppies as they romped playfully with their littermates. While the girls—frankly, I don't remember. It seems to me that they were more mature than the boys, socially *and* physically. Certainly they were better behaved. And I do remember that the best baseball player from our elementary school class attended John Muir. Her name was Marie.

"All right," Mr. Toomey said. "We're here to work."

We paid attention. I had never had a male teacher before. Neither had any of my friends. Mr. Toomey was tall and wiry with curly hair, perhaps thirty years of age. He had a face that looked like he might have been a boxer sometime in his life: a slightly flattened nose, thick earlobes, and skin that looked as tough as rhinoceros hide. He sounded tough. He meant business.

"How many of you can diagram a sentence?" We weren't sure we even knew what a sentence was. "Well then, who knows the principal parts of speech?" Still no hands.

Then the lectures and the drills began. By God, we were going to know this as well as we knew our names. Nouns, verbs, pronouns, adjectives, adverbs. Subject, object, predicate. Diagrams showed us the structure and relationship of sentences. Now that I think of it, they are not unlike a genealogical chart.

We sweated and groaned and complained. Mr. Toomey was a slave driver. A Captain Bligh. We had classroom exercises to hand in almost every day. Red-marked papers were handed back to students reluctant to see the measure of their failure. Split that infinitive. Forget that comma. Tote that barge. Lift that bale. Make a little mistake and you're gonna fail. Ugh!

Our escape was the playground. A hard game of basketball on an asphalt court would burn off all that bottled up energy and frustration.

My friend Jimmy Molyneaux, who, like me, was one of the smallest boys, was a whiz at basketball. He was fast and shifty, with a one-handed push shot that sent the ball toward the hoop as if drawn by a magnet. He lived even farther from school than I did, past our little apartment, so we walked to and from school together along the sidewalks of Vermont Avenue and onto Slauson Avenue, which paralleled the railroad tracks that ran alongside a mix of warehouses and commercial buildings.

Later on, when we were big eighth graders and I had moved, we were still pals. We were members of after-school athletic teams, the peewee league for little guys that played a succession of sports in season. I'm sure the intent was to keep us off the streets and out of trouble. It worked.

About that time Jimmy and I had started to notice girls. We both had a crush on the same girl, Katie Jenkins. I think that kept us together, watching to see that the other did not gain an advantage. Or perhaps to share fantasies, for alas, she barely took notice of either of us. She had a boyfriend whose father owned the fruit and vegetable concession at the local supermarket. It was rumored that this boy got an allowance of five dollars a week! Good grief! How could you compete with that when it was all you could do to scrape up a quarter from mowing a neighbor's lawn on Saturday?

There were other diversions on the playground. Another friend, Len Ash, was also a little guy. I don't know what it was about the smallest boys in our class, but they seemed to share an abnormal drive, the need to prove themselves. Jimmy was an outstanding athlete. I was the student. And Len—well, Len was Len.

I have known Len since I was six years old, and we still exchange Christmas cards and notes seventy-five years later. As a boy he reminded me of a young Mickey Rooney: a short, intense, feisty little guy with incredible energy.

For some reason one boy in our class raised Len's hackles. I never knew why. He was one of the bigger boys, a solid, thick kid almost a foot taller than Len. Every once in awhile—perhaps on the day of the full moon—Len would walk up to his nemesis and spit in his face. Just like that.

"Hey!" someone would shout. "They're at it again!" Then one of the kiss asses would run toward the shop building or the boys' gym looking for a teacher.

It was usually over before a teacher showed up. Len would bully and punch his opponent who, if he had had a mean streak, could have pulverized my friend. If a teacher didn't show up in time, the bell would ring, ushering us to our next class. At least, thank God, it would not be back to Mr. Toomey and English. Give us something simple—like math or science or Latin.

7

We survived a year of Mr. Toomey—and learned in spite of ourselves. Mrs. Heidergutt was still a year in the future. In the meantime my family had moved to our house on 59th Street, three blocks from school.

It was a neighborhood of frame and stucco houses, built in the 1920s, with decently kept green lawns with a mix of working class and middle class neighbors. A solid, New Deal, vote-for-FDR neighborhood. The country wasn't out of the Depression yet—it would take World War II to do that—but people seemed to be getting along.

Next door on one side lived the childless couple who owned two dry cleaning shops. On the other side lived Major MacDonald and his wife. He had retired from the Army after being in charge of the mess at West Point, the highlight of his career. I never heard him talk about World War I, which had been just twenty years prior. He was a big, genial, thoroughly nice Irish-American from New York with an equally friendly, almost childlike wife. When Major MacDonald died a few years later, Mrs. MacDonald would be found wandering the streets in confusion and tears, a lost soul.

Across the street lived Joanna Chlarson, a flaming redhead my sister's age whose father was a housepainter. Next door to her was Mrs. Heisenbuttle, a crippled, white-haired widow. Since she did not move around readily, Mrs. H. delighted in sitting bright-eyed on her front porch watching the doings of the neighborhood, especially the young people with all their energy and goings-on. She said it reminded her of when she was young. When we would stop by to chat, her wrinkled little hand would hold onto the sleeve of a blouse or a shirt to keep us from leaving too soon.

My closest neighborhood pals were two brothers, Mickey and Ralph Laszlo (their stepfather's surname). Mr. Laszlo was an entrepreneur who parlayed a string of vending machines into more successful businesses. Mickey and Ralph would later change their names back to the original Ledeaux, their father's name and a reminder of their Louisiana French heritage. On rainy days we would sit in their garage playing Monopoly, sampling the vending-machine peanuts stored there.

I had my school and church friends in addition to my neighborhood friends. Even now it amazes me to think about how children reach out into the world, unafraid and trusting. Although it can be intimidating to meet strangers, there is a certain radar that tells you when you meet a new friend. I went unselfconsciously into the world, with never a thought of rejection and so encountered none. Children, for the most part, are very accepting.

In the neighborhood you got to be friends . . . well, because you were there. When you're not near the people you like, you like the people you're near. When it comes to hide-and-seek or kick-the-can, the more the merrier.

Church was like that too. To the proximity—Sundays only, for the most part—was added the sharing of common faith. Onward Catholic soldiers! It didn't matter how your last name was spelled—most were Irish—because you had something in common greater than that. After the Sunday children's Mass there would be catechism class for those who did not attend parochial school. Here they fused those bonds of faith and togetherness.

"Who made the world?"

"God made the world."

"Who is God?"

"God is the creator of heaven and earth and of all things."

The nuns produced rewards when we knew our lesson: wallet-sized holy pictures of the Sacred Heart of Jesus or the Blessed Mother; cloth scapulars strung on leather cords to be worn around the neck and under the clothes until the cord rotted and broke or the holy picture on the small cloth square was obliterated by dirt and grime.

"As Catholics you should marry within the faith." Eyes glanced surreptitiously around the room. A few giggles, a guffaw or two. Oh, my. The brainwashing starts early.

But public school was different. Maybe proximity could be a factor. Especially if you sat next to a cute girl. And the only common faith was the belief that the bell would ring promptly at three o'clock so you could escape this purgatory.

The two main threads from which friendships were woven, at least for boys, were sports and grades. If you were good at sports, everybody wanted you to be on their team in PE class or after school. If you got good grades, you earned a certain respect and notoriety, as long as you weren't a teacher's pet, kiss ass, or grind. Not to speak of the occasional desperate whisper during an exam, "Psst. Candelaria. What's the answer to number four?"

Unlike neighborhood or church or summer visits to Albuquerque where I shared common blood with my cousins, public school opened the world to me. There was my friend Dave Wright, a redhead whose grandparents came from England and who reveled in books by H. Rider Haggard or about Lawrence of Arabia. There was my friend Len Ash, whose father came over on the boat from England as a young man. A Jew from England! That was a revelation. There were Protestants of all shapes, sizes, and ancestry. There were my Sephardic friends who spoke Spanish better than I did, only they called it Ladino.

One of the most delightful football seasons of that period was when I played halfback for two sandlot teams. One day I would be on the team from St. Columcille's with my Catholic friends who had names like Ennis and Brennan and Campbell. The next day I would be with my friends in the AZA league, an organization for Jewish boys. Because I was a ringer, there was a crisis before the first AZA game. Calling a quick huddle, my friend Bob Bloch decided that I should adopt a pseudonym. Moisha Candleberg! The referee never understood why we were laughing so hard that we almost fumbled the kickoff.

So it was that the world opened up. Books, movies, friends. While in school the world of writing slipped unobserved into my life, the way so much that's important seems to creep up on you. Instead of just reading plays, our social studies teacher declared, we were going to write them. As far as I was concerned they were just new assignments.

I don't even remember that teacher's name, God bless her. Nor do I remember much about these so-called works of art. Except one. Vaguely. It had something to do with wanting to drop out of school and how important it was not to. I not only wrote but starred in this classroom epic—a budding playwright and actor at the age of twelve.

I'm sure this bit of scholastic propaganda warmed the cockles of the teacher's heart and probably bored the bejesus out of the students. I have no inkling where the idea came from. It was certainly not to butter up the teacher. Horrors! That was the last thing I would have done. Teachers were those distant figures of authority, the all-wise whom one avoided, not least because of the potential disdain from fellow students.

The idea for the play might have come from my parents. Not directly, since I seldom discussed school details with them, but indirectly. They both encouraged education, but for different reasons. My mother's was that she had quit school to go to work after the eighth grade. My father's was that he had taught school for a year in a little mountain village east of Albuquerque before deciding teaching was not for him. (But that's another story.)

I doubt that the play portended any future literary talent. I suspect that it was on par with my acting, of which I do remember one incident. At the high point of the play, calling together my most passionate dramatic abilities, I spoke my lines in a loud and forthright manner—and mugged ingloriously. I could see the teacher, standing in the back of the class with arms folded across her chest. She unfolded her arms and started to say something about, I'm certain, the inappropriateness of my facial expression. The laughter from the student audience exploded before she could speak. She waved a hand as if swatting a fly and refolded her arms in resignation. So much for art.

8

For short periods during those summers my world narrowed. It was a world of brown-skinned family where the adults spoke Spanish, especially if they didn't want my sister and me to know what they were saying. It was a world of country and dirt roads, of cousins our age who did not seem as worldly as we were. While to them we were, no doubt, those city cousins who were ignoramuses about country ways. The glorious thing was that the adults were so busy visiting with each other, they ignored us kids or occasionally even bribed us with some loose change to get lost, which we did with enthusiasm.

Those idyllic summer days reminded me of the photograph of my father, age 12, in worn shoes, bib overalls, and a battered felt hat taken in Los Candelarias in 1917. It was the inspiration for a section in my first published novel, *Memories of the Alhambra*:

> There were cornfields now. . . . Cornfields that ran past the little adobe house for a long distance to the river. From the edge of the field he could see above the rows of corn the cluster of cottonwood trees that lined the Rio Grande, the Río Bravo del Norte of history. The boy stood at the rise alongside the irrigation ditch, barefoot, his bib overalls faded and patched, a shapeless hat on his head.
>
> "Herminio!" A wave of arm toward the rustling sound of movement in the cornfield. Then the small boy emerged, a crafty smile on his face softly lit by the sun fading into dusk.
>
> "Old man Griego's melons are ripe," he winked.
>
> José looked around surreptitiously. "Shh," he said, then walked up to Herminio where their whispers could be heard only by each other.

"We can cut through the cornfield," Herminio said. "I have a beautiful one all picked out. As gorgeous as Lucy Gallegos's behind. Then we can cut back toward the river and have a swim before we have our feast."

"After dinner," José said. "I have my chores to do. I'll tell Mamá I'm going to your house to study."

"And I'll tell my old lady I'm going to your house to study. If she believes that, she'll believe anything."

Now he could smell distinctly the faint sweetness of the growing corn. The boy was moving, crouched between two rows, not as fast as running but not as slow as walking either. "Herminio!" The whispered call traveled a ghostly route and died in silence, unanswered. "Herminio!"

"Over here," the whispered answer finally came. "This way."

They were cutting across the fields now, picking their way through the barbed-wire fence that separated corn from melon. "There," Herminio said. "That one." Then an elbow to José's ribs. "Doesn't that look like Lucy Gallegos?"

Trying to suppress his laugh, José followed Herminio, who tucked the melon under his arm. The giggling Herminio tried to stuff down his own laugh and the pressure of the swallowed sound exploded into a high-pitched fart. Then Herminio dropped the melon and fell onto the ground laughing aloud, while José, beside himself, let out a loud whoop that seemed to travel through space toward the moon.

Then they were at the river, breathless from running, while they dropped off their overalls and slipped into the dark coolness of the water. Rio Grande. River of life. Feeder of cornfields. Sweetener of melons. Cooler of boys at the end of the hot summer days.

He could taste the sweet melon now. Juice running down his chin. Filling the stomach that seemed forever hungry, unfulfilled by beans and tortillas and chile. "Don't swallow the seeds," he warned the gluttonous Hermino. "They'll grow inside of you into a melon."

"I'd like to plant a seed inside Lucy Gallegos."

And their laughter echoed along the banks of the quiet river. Flowed with barely a ripple, following the flowing waters toward the south. Toward the river's home, its final resting place—the Gulf of Mexico.

9

In September 1940 I returned to my last year, the ninth grade, at John Muir Junior High School. All during that school year the country was moving inexorably toward World War II. The only time we students were conscious of it was when we had to report on current events in social studies class or when it intruded on our personal lives. An older brother or uncle might have been drafted. Someone who had been unemployed got a job in a defense plant. Or we went to the movies and were caught up in the propaganda films that were preparing the country for war. We would leave the theater vowing that we'd show those Germans and Japs.

The literary news of the ninth grade was that Katie Jenkins, the girl that Jimmy Molyneaux and I both had a crush on, was Nellie Naturalist. That was the pseudonym of the gossip columnist for our school paper whose identity would not be revealed until the end of the school year. Jimmy and I must have been pretty dull copy. Neither of us were targets of gossip, so our names never appeared in print.

The other event of excitement, aside from being promoted to high school at the end of the year, was joint weekly physical education sessions in the girls' gym. It was time to learn to dance so we wouldn't disgrace ourselves at the senior dance and to learn a little decorum in the presence of the opposite sex.

The dancing sessions were overseen by the girls' and boys' physical education teachers. One of the teachers would put a 78-rpm record on the player and out would come the music.

"All right, line up. Boys on the left; girls on the right. Now march across the gym in time to the music and halt as you approach your partner."

Giggle, giggle. Groan. God! Look who I got this time. Sweaty palms. Total loss of rhythm. Leaden feet. The inability to count.

I don't remember if they tried to teach us the fox-trot or the waltz. I do remember the two-step and one particular song that I can still hear in my nightmares. Hell is learning to do the two-step with the ugly, gum-chewing girl who has a crush on you while Raymond Scott and his quintet play "Huckleberry Duck." One, two. One, two. One leaden foot forward, then the other dragged next to it, like the sliding walk of one of those movie monsters in a horror flick. Igor with the clubfoot. Oh, God! I'd rather go to math than do this!

Except for these few highlights, school was an endless session of the mundane. Our English teacher, Mrs. Heidergutt, indoctrinated us with all the fervor of a missionary saving the heathen from a life of sin. Her method was total immersion. Each day ended with a short, intense series of exercises to be handed in, then returned corrected the next day. Woe be to anyone who failed to turn in his worksheet! A large N, for non-satisfactory, would be entered in that day's column in her black grade book. At the end of the semester a succession of Ns meant doom for your report card.

It was the teacher of another class, Mrs. Parker, who touched me with a feeling other than the fear of failure. I was a shy, well-behaved boy, socially less adept than my older classmates.

I don't remember all of the details, but I do know that we were filling out some kind of official form in our social studies class. No doubt it was something for the files in the school office. As on many such forms in those days there was a section labeled "Race," with little boxes alongside the words "White, Colored, Oriental. Check one."

For some reason, that day the question gave me pause. Perhaps it was the beginning of the loss of innocence. Or perhaps questions buried deep began to surface. I must have looked around the classroom in some confusion. I could see what white looked like. Then I looked down at my hand and wrist, perhaps remembering the sleepy face that stared back at me from the bathroom mirror that morning. Well, I certainly didn't look white.

I turned back to the words with little boxes alongside and put an X in the box beside the word *colored*.

I don't know how long Mrs. Parker might have been standing behind my desk. She may have just walked quietly down the aisle as I made that mark. A hand reached over my shoulder, gently took the pencil from my hand, turned it eraser downward, and erased the X. Then the pencil turned right side up and placed an X alongside the word *white*.

Not a word was spoken. I looked at the form, then at Mrs. Parker, who continued quietly down the aisle with not so much as a glance my way.

Later, toward the end of the semester, she and her student teacher, a young man, whose name I forget, spoke to me after class. "You must go to college, Nash," she said. The student teacher echoed her words.

I don't remember what I answered. Probably some mumbled words of agreement. I may have already had such ambitions. What I did know was that going to college was not the norm for this school and this neighborhood. A few might go on to junior college to take advanced courses in drafting or business so they could get better jobs in a defense plant or as a secretary. I remember feeling singled out, and I resolved that, yes, going to college would be the right thing to do.

Two years later, I passed by the junior high on my way home from high school, dressed in an ROTC uniform. It was 1943. The attack at Pearl Harbor had long since thrust us into World War II. There was no stigma to being in the ROTC as there was later during the Vietnam War. Quite the contrary.

A voice called out, "Nash!" as if in surprise. Perhaps at the uniform.

I turned my head and caught a glimpse of Mrs. Parker. I was overcome by an attack of shyness. I turned quickly and continued on my way. Only later, when I arrived home, did I suffer remorse for not stopping and talking to her. It's an omission I've regretted all of my life. I never saw her again.

10

I suppose two things during that last year of junior high school had bearing on my becoming a writer. The first was that during the ninth grade there was time to take an elective or two after completing courses required for college entrance. It was a relief after the straight dose of English, history, social studies, math, science, and foreign language.

My elective was typewriting. I have no idea why. It may have been that I got tired of writing school reports in longhand. Or that teachers graded papers for neatness as well as content, and I was competitive enough to want that edge. Or that my father had promised me a typewriter for Christmas if I did well in the class.

That Christmas I found an Underwood portable typewriter under the tree. The keys were capped in black so that the letters, numbers, and symbols were not visible. I had to practice the touch-typing system at home without the crutch of peeking at the keys. Little did I dream that later, in the era of computers, it would make that new skill easier to acquire. (In my business career, I knew corporate executives who resisted using computers because they had never learned to type.) But whoever heard of a computer in December 1940?

One of the few mementos from my early writing years surfaced after my mother died in 1982. I went through her effects like an archaeologist digging at the site of a lost world. Buried deep in one of the old boxes in the garage among my sister's and my ancient report cards and toys that mother had saved for her grandchildren, my sons, to play with when they came to visit, was an old report from the ninth grade, a shard of the creative writing activities of a twelve-year-old.

It was not, as you might expect, a remnant from English class. I was not on the staff of the school paper or a contributor to its occasional offerings of student creative writing. This was from history class, a report on the British navy.

Typed neatly in the back of the report, starting on page thirty-four, was an original problem. It was an appendix, probably written for extra credit, titled "Have You Done Your Duty? (A combined story and poem)." It was three pages, starting in rhyme that passed for poetry, then prose, extolling the bravery of a cabin boy who served with Admiral Nelson and was present at his death during the Battle of Trafalgar. The teacher gave it an A+.

My mother must have been impressed. She saved it along with other souvenirs of my sister's and my childhoods, to be discovered forty-two years later. I must confess that I read it with some amusement. What surprised me was how naturally that little brown-skinned boy projected himself onto the admiral's flagship, inspired no doubt by Hollywood actor Errol Flynn's swashbuckling his way through the movie *Captain Blood*.

It seemed proper to imagine himself as an English cabin boy with no sign of ethnic consciousness that might have suggested a more appropriate hero. Christopher Columbus. Ferdinand Magellan. Vasco Núñez de Balboa. Or whoever commanded the Spanish fleet during the battles of the Spanish Armada. But then, we were studying *English* history, and these were different times. Besides, in all those sea movies of that period, the Spanish were always the *bad* guys, as were the Mexicans in the cowboy flicks. Who wanted to be a bad guy?

Meanwhile, important decisions were being discussed by students. The most important: What high school would we attend? I lived in the George Washington High School District. Two neighboring students who lived on the next block were going there. I thought they were snobs. They kept themselves apart from other young people in the neighborhood. For what reason I didn't know. The only reason that I could see was that one of them lived in a stucco house while the rest of ours were frame. Big deal!

My junior high school friends would be scattering. Jimmy Molyneaux was going to Fremont High on the east side. A few were going to George Washington, which was south. Most of my friends were going to Manual Arts High School, one of the oldest in the city. It was the alma mater, we were to learn later, of World War II hero General James Doolittle, who led the first American bombing raid on Tokyo.

My heart said Manual Arts. What settled it was that Manual Arts had a Reserve Officers Training Corps program while George Washington did not. In the spring of 1941 our entry into World War II seemed only a matter of time. It was patriotic to be in ROTC. Obtaining permission to transfer schools in order to enroll in ROTC was a foregone conclusion.

11

While that was the end of my studies at John Muir Junior High School, it was not the end of that school in my life. My sister, Lillian, who was a year and five months younger than I, followed. Rumors spread among the students the year after I graduated that someone had just completed the ninth grade at an incredibly young age. Typical was fourteen or fifteen. Like all such rumors there was less truth than exaggeration and gossip to it. I had turned thirteen the month before graduation.

This was but one of the crosses Lillian had to bear as my younger sister. Perhaps typical was her experience in math class. She had the fortune, or misfortune, to have the same teacher that I had had, Miss Corley. Miss Corley was a rather severe-looking spinster. She did not suffer nonsense in her class; she was in charge. But underneath she was a kindly, helpful person.

Math must have been one of my better subjects because I remember that when she had to leave the room for short periods of time she would leave me in charge to continue with the lesson. She tried to draw me out of my shyness and the wall that existed between me and the adult teachers. One Saturday she asked me to come to her house and do some yard work for her, which I did quietly and efficiently. However, it did not result in any transition toward loquaciousness.

At the time Lillian was assigned to Miss Corley's class, there was another Candelaria in the school—not related—by the name of Leroy. Leroy was a kid notorious in his own right for truancy and fighting and was headed for reform school, according to some teachers. He eventually found his way to what is now called continuation school, the place for problem students, with truancy being one of the main problems. When Miss Corley asked Lillian if she was Nash's sister, it was more than she could bear. That goody-goody little Nash! "No!" she replied. "I'm Leroy's sister!"

Another incident occurred sometime later. Lillian was running for an office in student government, either girls' vice president or secretary. The standard forums for campaigning for school office were two assemblies in the school auditorium, one for the seventh and lower eighth grades, and the other for the upper eighth and ninth grades.

This was a time of great racial unrest in Los Angeles and surrounding communities, especially in the Spanish-speaking barrios on the east side. Then as now, Los Angeles had the largest population of people of Mexican descent of any city in the United States. Newspapers headlined the Sleepy Lagoon murder and the racist trial in which several young Chicanos were convicted on questionable circumstantial evidence.

Young Mexican American males, many second generation in this country, were looked down upon, jobless, and misunderstood. They affected distinction with their zoot suits: knee-length coats, peg-top pants, watch chains that hung down to their ankles. Underneath their broad-brimmed hats were their ducktail haircuts. When you think about the exaggerated costumes and hairdos of young mainstream Americans since that time, you wonder what the fuss was about, although hair did become a symbol for violent reaction in the 1960s.

Many of these pachucos organized in neighborhood clubs or gangs—the choice of word often depending on your point of view. *Gang,* then as now, had the connotation of crime and gangsters, whereas clubs, of course, are as American as apple pie: boys clubs, athletic clubs, country clubs.

There's no denying the hoodlum activities of some of these young men. There had been incidents of sailors robbed as well as knifed in fights with zoot-suited gangs. Many young Chicanos, however, were guilty only of wearing the exaggerated costume.

It was in such a climate that the political campaign in this junior high school, far removed from the troubled barrios, was held. Lillian's feelings about Miss Corley found their way into her political speech. Onstage during the first assembly, she reached the climax of her pitch, ending it with a declaration of her ability to serve in that office. She called on her nemesis, Miss Corley, for verification: "Isn't that right, Miss Corley?" Whereupon she lifted a hand from her side and aimed a toy water pistol, out in plain view, toward the audience.

The students cheered and stomped. The faculty was stunned. In a quick conference before the second assembly, Lillian's water pistol was appropriated. She was asked to tone down what the administration saw as an inflammatory speech, and her second appearance in front of a student audience lacked the gun moll bravado of her first. Notwithstanding, she won the election.

Six months later, in the summer of 1943, the situation in Los Angeles exploded into the infamous Zoot Suit Riots when vigilante servicemen marched the streets with chains and clubs looking for zoot-suiters. Police cars followed caravans of sailors and soldiers. Zoot-suiters were dragged from downtown movie theatres and off streetcars and were beaten and stripped of their clothes. The police, who watched the beatings, then arrested the victims while the shore patrol and military police seemed disinterested or made futile attempts to curb military personnel.

Suspicion and ill will were fed by inflammatory headlines in local newspapers, such as the *Los Angeles Examiner,* the *Herald & Express,* and the *Los Angeles Times.* Some headlines, like the *Examiner's* "Police Must Clean Up L.A. Hoodlumism," referred to zoot-suiters, not to servicemen.

Even Chicanos not living in the barrio felt the stultifying effect of official and community attitudes. The legacy of Rodney King goes back to Watts and the Zoot Suit Riots, echoing conditions and attitudes that have changed little over the years.

12

High school was another broadening of horizons for me. Manual Arts High School was at 42nd Street and Vermont Avenue. It was not far from the campus of the University of Southern California (USC) and from the Los Angeles Memorial Coliseum, built for the 1932 Olympic Games.

Like many a schoolboy sports fanatic, I was well acquainted with the coliseum. In football season some of the young neighborhood athletes would take the streetcar to the stadium where we would hire out to sell newspapers before and after the game. While the money was OK—two cents a paper—the real incentive was the game itself. After we sold our quota of newspapers before the game, we were allowed in to see the contest for free. Free! The one condition was that we had to leave at the end of the third quarter and get ready to sell newspapers to the departing crowd.

Unfortunately, there came a Saturday when I suffered an acute dilemma. It was one of the games in the famous rivalry between USC and Notre Dame. All my church friends were there, true sidewalk alumni of the Fighting Irish. It was a titanic battle where the issue was in doubt to the very end. At the beginning of the fourth quarter I suffered an attack of conscience—for a millisecond. Caught up in the frenzy of the crowd cheering for old Notre Dame, I stayed the entire fourth quarter, my heart pounding, as I rooted for our team—"Beat 'em, Irish!"—only to face the irate newspaper supervisor on my way out. "You're fired!" he roared. "Don't bother to come back!"

Although I was familiar with the neighborhood, I had never been on the Manual Arts campus itself. It was bigger by far than John Muir Junior High School. In the entering class alone there were 500 students from several junior high schools. It was a mainstream student body. There were a few Mexican American students, a few African Americans, fewer Chinese Americans, and some Japanese American students who, along with their families, would soon disappear into government concentration camps.

We hardly realized at the start of the school year how soon the war would change our lives. A new school—*high* school—was exciting. We were mature, almost adult, *high* school students, but we bore some anxiety for what lay ahead. Fortunately, our uncertainty and fear of being alone in a new school faded when we encountered old familiar faces, old friends, from junior high.

My homeroom teacher was Miss Addison, who would later also be my eleventh grade English teacher. She was one of those spinster teachers—there seemed to be many of them at that time—married to her work. In the fall of 1941 she must have been in her fifties, a stout gray-haired woman who, I remember, wore severely tailored navy blue suits with skirts that hung down to her ankles.

She was a declaimer who loved to read to her students. She would stand in front of the class like a Roman orator inciting a crowd or like a Victorian actress on stage. "Friends, Romans, students, lend me your ears." Later, in her English class, she subjected us to the likes of *Silas Marner* and *The Mill on the Floss*. It was enough to poison the joy of reading for many a resistant student.

The big excitement for many of us, though, was ROTC, the reason I was attending Manual Arts and not Washington High School. The class was offered in place of physical education. This automatically separated the jocks from the rotsies. Some of the jocks would become high school heroes because of their prowess at football, basketball, or track. The rotsies appealed to student patriotism because of the war then raging in Europe and sympathy for our allies fighting Hitler and Mussolini.

One of the incentives for being a "rotsy" was the uniform. I don't mean the appeal that uniforms had for some of the girls, although there was an ROTC ball every year that high school girls clamored to attend in their formal gowns. No, the real incentive was the money your family saved on clothes since you had to wear a wool uniform three days a week (Monday through Wednesday). For growing boys who were hard on jeans and had families who barely made ends meet, this was a boon. From top to toe, the only item you had to buy was underwear (which nobody saw anyway so who cared how patched and ragged or whether you wore any at all), shoes, and socks. The rest was GI: cap, shirt, necktie, trousers, belt, and on Wednesdays, which were full-dress days, a coat.

Manual Arts High School ROTC, circa 1942.
Nash is second from left; Leonard Ash is far left.

While jocks ran up and down the field or court, rotsies practiced close order drill, marching at right shoulder arms with .30 caliber Springfield 1903 rifles that had seen better days during World War I. While jocks had their weekly game against rival teams, rotsies marched in full dress to the accompaniment of the ROTC band. And while coaches instructed jocks in the rules of the game and winning strategies, rotsies were instructed in military theory, including map reading, using a compass, belly crawling (heading out to no-man's land), and practice on the rifle range under the bleachers with .22 caliber rifles and live ammunition.

One advantage that jocks had was in laundry and upkeep. Gym clothes could lie in lockers until they became ripe enough to erupt into bacterial cultures or until the aroma, unnoticed by students, became strong enough to walk and some teacher threatened to notify the sanitation department. Laundry of game uniforms was the responsibility of the school.

Rotsies, on the other hand, were mired in discipline that was exacted in spit and polish. There were brass buttons on dress coats, insignia on caps, and belt buckles—all to be gone over with a glad rag containing polish that, if you used it hard enough, made brass shine like a mirror. There were shoes and leather belts to be shined, and rotsies with the shiniest leather jealously kept secret the name of the polish that gave such brilliant results. But most challenging of all were the cotton shirts. They had to be starched, then ironed with two creases down the front and three in the back, straight and stiff enough to cut paper. My mother refused to iron them so I had to learn to do it myself, especially since our uniforms were inspected every day and with even greater scrutiny on full-dress days.

Successful athletic teams would compete in league playoffs that ultimately determined the contest for city championships. ROTC battalions competed with those of other schools for city championships in massive parades in the coliseum. Jocks who met the requirements earned purple school letters that could be sewed onto gray letterman sweaters, walking advertisements of a student's athletic prowess. Rotsies who marched and drilled exception-ally earned ribbons for best private and best platoon as well as awards for sharpshooting—these to be worn on the breasts of uniform coats.

The jocks had their coaches, ex-college athletes, some of whom had reputations for being tough and demanding. Rotsies had one full-time instructor, Sergeant Backell. A career army man in his mid-thirties, he had close-cropped, sandy hair and eyeglass lenses as thick as the bottoms of Coke bottles, which, we agreed, kept him out of combat duty. He dealt with this ragtag army of high school boys with a firm hand but with understanding and a certain sense of humor. One of the pleasures of being one of Sergeant Backell's boys was to hang around the ROTC office during free time and listen to him spin old war stories. This was the real stuff!

Once a week Sergeant Backell's superior, Captain Nagelman, came in to inspect the troops. A handsome man with a dapper mustache, he had several high schools under his jurisdiction, so he left the day-to-day details to subordinates like Sergeant Backell. His inspections seemed cursory. He didn't seem too interested in the students, although he did take to a few, usually the wilder and more aggressive cadets. Perhaps he saw in them candidates for leading charges out of trenches into enemy territory.

ROTC was exciting for the cadets in the corps. It gave us a chance to learn skills that would stand us in good stead when it was our turn to serve in the army. We were future leaders in the defense of democracy. It enabled us to show our patriotism and support for older brothers, uncles, and cousins who were already in the military.

Three months later, December 7, 1941, this boyish innocence of ours was to collide with reality.

13

There are events in life that remain vivid forever. Although I was only five at the time, I clearly remember the Long Beach earthquake of 1933. We were living in a little frame house in Los Angeles on 47th Street near Broadway. My sister and I were playing in the yard with neighbor children, and someone, I forget who, had just climbed down from a tree. Suddenly the earth moved with a terrifying shudder and threw us to the ground. Then it was over abruptly, leaving a stillness that was almost as frightening as the shake.

My mother's younger brother, my Uncle Albert, was staying with us at the time, having come from Albuquerque to look for work. He came running out the front door of the house, wet, dressed only in a bath towel wrapped around his waist. Albert, who must have been about nineteen or twenty years old then, had been soaking in the tub recuperating from a hangover. He thought the world was coming to an end.

Sunday, December 7, 1941, was another day that I'll always remember. We received word about the Japanese attack on Pearl Harbor about noon that day; it must have been after coming home from Mass. I can still hear the voice of President Franklin Delano Roosevelt crackling over the radio the following day as he asked Congress to declare war: "Yesterday, December 7, 1941—a date which will live in infamy—the United States of America was suddenly and deliberately attacked by naval and air forces of the Empire of Japan."

But on that Sunday there were news flashes over the radio. We were stunned, listening in silence to the reports. Like all families, we had loved ones in the military. My Uncle Albert had been drafted and spent much of the war on army duty in the Aleutian Islands. His older brother, my Uncle Henry, was in the army. He was later to be offered a field promotion to lieutenant, which he refused, preferring to serve as a noncombatant medic.

On my father's side of the family, there were two first cousins old enough to serve. Both my cousins Peter Griego and Louis Candelaria completed their studies at the University of New Mexico and entered the military—Louis for training as a bombardier officer in the Army Air Corps, and Peter to become an artillery officer.

I can remember our father barking orders at my sister and me, telling us what a tough marine sergeant he'd make if he were in the service. Snap to! Make your bed! Do the dishes! Hut! Two! Three! Four! He was thirty-six at the time, with a wife, a twelve-year-old daughter, and a thirteen-year-old son, definitely not what the recruiters were looking for.

After hearing the news, I remember going outside and meeting my friends Mickey and Ralph. We sat on the steps of our house talking seriously about what had happened.

"We'll beat them in six months!" I remember saying, indignant at the treachery and audacity of the Japanese government and military. I was too much taken with my three months of ROTC training and the wartime propaganda movies I had seen.

No, both Mickey and Ralph insisted. It was going to take longer. It was going to be tough. I don't know where they got their information. Presumably from their stepfather, who had been born in Hungary, which had been overpowered by Hitler as German forces marched through to Yugoslavia. Their stepfather knew something about the Germans and the Italians and, by inference, about their Japanese allies. He better sensed their strength and their intent and saw the war for the desperate, difficult struggle it would be.

Shortly after, Japanese American students began to disappear from school. Such was the xenophobia of the times that later, at the time of the Zoot Suit Riots in Los Angeles, an article in *Time* magazine stated:

> The overwhelming majority of Americans (67%) feel that they can get along considerably better with Germany than with Japan after the war, the Gallup Poll reported last week. The pollsters documented U.S. hate for Japan by jotting down the adjectives citizens applied to the Jap: "Barbaric, evil, brutal, dirty, treacherous, sneaky, fanatical, savage, inhuman, bestial, uncivilized, un-Christian and thoroughly untrustworthy."
>
> "Other terms used," added the Gallup Poll, "are unprintable."

At the same time, during the Sleepy Lagoon murder trial in Los Angeles, a sheriff's department expert on foreign relations assessed Americans of Mexican descent this way:

> "Let us view it from the biological basis. . . . Total disregard for human life has always been universal throughout the Americas in the human population. And this Mexican element feels a desire to kill or at least to draw blood."

Later, my parents would talk in hushed tones about the New Mexico National Guard, boys from back home who had been serving in the Philippines and had been captured by the Japanese. They were among the 40,000 U.S. troops who suffered the Bataan Death March, seventy miles of hell on the way to prison camps during which half of them died. Nine hundred of the dead had been boys from New Mexico.

Early during the war the Pacific Coast, from California to Washington, was in a state of anxiety about a possible Japanese invasion. Homes had blackout curtains and there were a few air raid alarms, the wail of ghostly sirens telling us to turn out all lights while high above in the night search-lights cut the black sky, hunting for enemy airplanes.

Only two months after Pearl Harbor, a Japanese submarine a mile offshore shelled an oil refinery just north of Santa Barbara. Later that fall a Japanese navy airplane dropped incendiary bombs on an Oregon forest, on a mission to start a fire.

Things at Manual Arts High School changed, as they did in the country at large. There was a seriousness and purpose to our daily lives. There was rationing to contend with, sugar and gasoline being the two that made most impact on me. There were scrap metal and paper drives. People collected cooking grease and tin foil saved from chewing gum wrappers and cigarette packs. Families planted victory gardens to supplement their diets. And there were war bond drives with students buying stamps and saving them in book-lets until they had $18.75 for a war bond redeemable in ten years for $25.00.

The war colored our entire three years of high school. People made whatever contribution they could on the home front, while others served in the military. My friend Dave Wright, who had been gravely ill as a boy and missed a year of school, did not get to graduate with our class. He had been drafted into the army at eighteen. Other boys dropped out of school to enlist in the navy. A few girls—very few, since these were different times—blossomed out pregnant, farewell gifts from their boyfriends who had gone to serve their country and who possibly never would be seen alive again.

And in my senior year there was a tragedy that shook the entire school. Bob Simonian, an extremely popular young man who was a favorite with students and teachers alike and a young man of great promise—cheerleader, student body president of the year just past—had been killed in combat. He was nineteen years old.

14

Such was the climate in Los Angeles during my high school days, a mixture of patriotic resolve and xenophobia. If war can excuse killing, racist attitudes toward people who are different is but a venial sin—or no sin at all. Of course, I didn't see that as a boy. It was all right to hate the Japs. We were fighting them. But Mexicans were something else. After all, these were people who lived in the United States, many of them American citizens.

There was one way to sidestep the issue: we could remember that we were Spanish. My parents talked in hushed tones to adult cousins and friends whom we visited in the barrios of Boyle Heights and East L.A.

"Gangs," they said. Whisper, whisper, whisper. Their anxieties were palpable. They were afraid that their children might be attacked by gangs, or even *join* one.

And that summer in Los Candelarias, I can remember walking a dirt country road with two male cousins who were about my age. We passed open fields and an occasional adobe house. A small boy, smaller than any of us, stepped onto the road from one of the houses. He walked up to my oldest cousin, the biggest of the three of us, doubled up a fist, and hit him in the stomach.

I was shocked and ready to retaliate. My cousin, grimacing from the blow, put out a hand to restrain me. "No," he said.

He tossed his head to the side, pointing toward the house. Sitting on the dirt, leaning against the wall, was a boy a few years older than we were. He looked up through threatening narrowed eyes, all the time whittling on a piece of wood with a long-bladed knife.

"That's his brother," my cousin said, meaning the smaller boy who had hit him.

Still later that vacation the three of us went to a dance in the neighboring farm area of Alameda. I noticed a particularly pretty girl across the dance floor and pointed her out to my cousin. "I think I'll go ask her to dance," I said.

Once again my cousin cautioned me. "No," he said. "She's got a jealous boyfriend. He has a knife." All I could think was: What's the point of going to a dance if you can't ask a girl to dance?

For all of this, I seemed to walk obliviously through life, untouched for the most part by what was happening in the barrios of Los Angeles. Yet something had to be going on deep inside. It was not anything I could talk about, because I wasn't conscious of it myself.

I felt a certain superiority that I could speak English without an accent, unlike some of my cousins. I can remember reading in a biology or anthropology book about a Caucasian earlobe trait known as a Darwin's point. I noticed in the mirror with some relief that there was such a point on my left ear.

Then, of course, like most teenagers, I became more critical of my father. My sister and I reacted intensely to the old-fashioned way he combed his hair, parted down the middle, the 1920s and early 1930s way. After he had a beer or two and his longish hair became disheveled, it hung in his face, giving him the look of a Mexican bandido. I did not see that I was a true son of my father: dark eyes, dark hair, large head, dark complexion, a hint of the Pueblos. All I knew was that I didn't like the way he looked. As for myself, all I saw was a Darwin's point and a desire to be accepted, a desire *not* to be different.

15

Looking back, one of the ways that I reacted to the social climate was in my drive to excel. It was unconscious. It was like an invisible burr under the saddle that propelled me full speed ahead. I learned early that there was virtue in being the best or one of the best students in class. It was a sign of being above reproach. It granted me immunity from some of the prevailing attitudes about Mexicans—about being different. It also was good old American competitiveness.

Among schoolmates we were all equal, all the same. At least on the surface, color, ancestry, and religion seemed of little concern except to a very few snobs. The measure of fellow students was how well they performed in class or in athletics—and their friendliness and approachability. On the other hand, being too friendly with teachers or being a grind who did nothing but study were major transgressions. "Kiss ass" and "grind" were words almost on a par with "Jap" or "Nazi."

Part of this attitude toward performance may have been that only a few minority students attended Manual Arts High School, and most of them were good students or athletes or were gifted in music. In a city where school population was determined by the makeup of neighborhoods, these minority students had come from families that were, in the truest sense, pioneers. Los Angeles at that time was a ghettoized city—as it probably still is. Housing may not have been overtly segregated by law, but in essence that's the way things worked out.

Mexican American students for the most part attended schools on the eastside like Roosevelt High. Black students usually went to Jefferson High. Jewish students made up a large part of the population of westside Fairfax High. Troublemakers, of whatever description, were sent to that day's equivalent of continuation school, Jacob Riis High, unless they dropped out of school. While the rest went to other schools, including the more affluent mostly lily-white schools like Los Angeles High or University High.

Those of us at Manual Arts High were like a small sprinkling of pepper in a large shaker of salt. In such a large shaker, a little pepper was hardly noticed. This made it more palatable to salt lovers. The only ethnic incident that I remember in my three years of high school was a report that the older brother of a popular student in my class had greatly upset his family because he was going to marry an *Italian* girl. You can imagine what they must have thought about Mexicans!

In such an atmosphere, a grain of pepper might not even realize it was pepper. That's how it must have been in my case. I did not consciously choose my friends because they were *like* me or *unlike* me—this, that, or the other. It just happened. Because of the war, ROTC cadets tended to hang out together. I also had my friends from junior high, many of whom were not in ROTC, as well as new friends. Some of these were rivals for grades, and we shared a wary, mutual respect more than heartfelt warmth.

One of my pals at the time was Phil Mannion, who had recently moved into our neighborhood, was in my grade, and was also a member of the ROTC. Each morning I would walk the block and a half to the small cottage where he lived with his mother and his older sister, Molly. I would knock on the door, often waking him, and hustle him down to Vermont Avenue and the streetcar stop. After school we would walk the twenty or so blocks home together.

Thus it was that I lived school life in the mainstream world, like a fish unconscious of the water in which it swam. For a short time each summer I would visit that other world, the narrow world of farm country Albuquerque. It was not incongruous to partake of two different worlds. It seemed quite natural, and I hardly thought about it. But the first glimmer of this schism finally came to me in a high school music class.

I don't recall what the special occasion was, but the class was learning the Spanish-language song, "Las Mañanitas." The teacher wanted someone to read the lyrics aloud so the class could learn the proper pronunciation.

There were two of us with surnames that implied that we might be of help: Walter Acosta and myself. Walter was a fair-skinned, brown-haired student who could have passed for one of my gringo-looking Dalton cousins.

I was asked to read first. I stumbled over the words like a tongue-twisted gringo, and I could see the judgment and disappointment on the teacher's face. Then Walter read beautifully. He had a rich voice, and it was obvious that he spoke Spanish well because his pronunciation was flawless.

I could have died of embarrassment from my poor performance. My parents' efforts to have my sister and me speak only English had worked too well. I was, in a sense, culturally deprived. I was what the more militant Chicanos would later refer to with derision as a coconut: brown on the outside and white on the inside.

Another incident in art class the next year also affected me, but somewhat differently. Someone had a charro suit, and I was asked to model it as the rest of the class drew me. The costume included tight black trousers with silver piping down the sides, a short black embroidered jacket, a white shirt with lacy collar, a large black sombrero with silver embroidery, to which someone contributed a guitar. I hated it! What did this Mexican cowboy suit have to do with me? My heritage was *New* Mexican. We were poor farmers who never wore charro suits. We had been Americans for a hundred years. Besides, the damned wool suit itched as I sat posing through several days of warm weather.

Other than that, it was school as usual. Those of us on the academic track took college preparatory courses in math, chemistry, and—the most challenging—physics. I bumped head-on into the boundaries of my ignorance, like not knowing what *Time* magazine was when it was discussed in social studies. My parents didn't read *Time* magazine. My parents couldn't afford *Time* magazine. Yet I responded to the challenges as best I could, with few signs evident of the writer I would eventually become.

16

The students at Manual Arts High School did their share during the war. One of the major events occurred in 1943, when I was in the eleventh grade. It was a huge war bond drive, emulating those highly publicized efforts by Hollywood movie stars and other public personalities.

Students went out into the community to get family, friends, and neighbors to pledge to buy bonds to help finance the war. I don't recall the exact monetary goal, but it must have been an ambitious one. There were other activities too, such as a scrap metal collection, during which one enterprising young student managed to bring in an abandoned automobile.

To whip up enthusiasm and harness student energy, awards were given for outstanding efforts—such as growing the best victory garden. Naturally, budding young salespeople strove to see who could solicit pledges for the greatest number of war bonds, and students helped promote efforts by creating posters that were displayed on campus.

While I didn't know it at the time, this was the occasion of my introduction to creative writing in high school. Like many important things in our lives, it was fortuitous, something that sneaked up on me when I was looking the other way.

It happened in study hall, the free period every student had each day during which we were supposed to study. It was a large group of students, perhaps two or three times as many as in a regular class, monitored by a single teacher. The room was a beehive of whispering, note passing, reading comic books in preference to schoolbooks, and a few well-behaved souls who actually studied.

Mr. Arons, our study hall teacher, kept the class in better order than most. He taught physical education and coached the gymnastics team. Although one of his legs was crippled so that he walked with a jerky motion, his gymnast arm muscles bulged through the short sleeves of his gray flannel gym shirt and no one questioned his authority.

He spent most of study hall walking slowly around the room, his mere presence keeping down the noise level and intimidating a few to study who otherwise would be goofing off. He also taught math classes and would occasionally stop and answer a question for a student about their math homework.

One day he announced to the class that as part of the war bond drive there was to be a slogan contest. He asked for volunteers to contribute entries. As he looked around the class, the response was underwhelming. It may have also been one of those days that students were more unruly than usual. For whatever reason, our lack of patriotic fervor did not sit well with Mr. Arons.

"All right!" he snapped. "I want each of you to write a slogan and hand it to me before you leave study hall today!"

Groans and moans. A slogan! How do you write a slogan?

I was one of those students who liked to race through his homework during study hall so I would have little or none to do at home that night. There were other things to do after school. Play with friends. Go out to the park. Listen to the radio. This slogan business was just another one of those unwelcome interruptions.

I gave the slogan the little time I thought it deserved. I must have stared in the air a few minutes waiting for the muse. Perhaps I remembered the poem-story from ninth grade about the gallant cabin boy and Admiral Nelson, and the rhythm of the words triggered something. Whatever heaven or hell it came from, the words popped out, and I wrote them down quickly:

> Beat the Axis;
> Do your share.
> Bonds and stamps
> Will pay your fare.

Some days later Mr. Arons announced proudly that one of his students had won the slogan contest: Me! What a surprise! There was to be a general student body awards assembly sponsored by the U.S. Marine Corps. Entertainment would be by the popular radio and recording star Spike Jones and his orchestra, whose comic wartime recording "Der Fuhrer's Face" satirized the Nazis in an effort to boost American morale.

At the assembly, which was held in the school auditorium, Spike Jones and his crew took to the stage with the instruments they played during their comic numbers: a washboard, cowbells, a revolver with blank cartridges (or it may have been a very loud cap pistol), and various other unmusical noisemakers.

The MC was a public information officer, a captain in the Marine Corps who had been a radio announcer in civilian life. Students who were to receive awards had been given typed scripts from which to read since the program was being recorded for radio broadcast later.

The entertainment came first. The Spike Jones orchestra played some of their zany numbers. Their singer, Jones's wife, Helen Greyco, had her time on stage. Two students, Houghton and Hecht, did the act they had performed during student talent shows. Dressed in their ROTC uniforms (what else?) they sang their rendition of the Spike Jones hit:

When der Fuhrer says
Ve is der master race,
Ve heil! Pttt! Heil! Pttt!
Right in der Fuhrer's face.

The sound effect *Pttt*, of course, was a Bronx cheer with an accompanying Nazi salute.

Then were the awards. Sixty years later I can still picture two of the student winners, but I don't remember their names. The award for most war bond pledges was won by a tall, gawky young student, a fellow ROTC member who was in the tenth grade. He had hustled an outrageous number of war bonds—I want to say $50,000 worth, but it very well may have been $5,000. The other winner that I remember was a tall black girl who had done something special with victory gardens. She stood proudly with the quiet dignity of a Marian Anderson.

Then my turn came to exchange banter with the MC and receive my award. I turned to the MC and said:

"I once won five dollars for saying just five letters."

Surprise. "Oh? What was that?"

"B-I-N-G-O!"

When the laughter died, I got to read my slogan. Oh, to be fourteen years old when the world is your oyster. Would it ever be that good again?

17

That summer, after I finished the eleventh grade, I got my first real job. Not that there hadn't been jobs before; I had worked the usual kind held by Depression kids who didn't know what allowances were. Even parents who were lucky enough to have jobs—and my father had a civil service job where the great virtue was its permanence—rarely had extra money for allowances. We were a younger version of those unemployed hordes: on the dole, badgering mom or dad for a dime to go to the movies. Sometimes it worked.

When we were living in Albuquerque and I was seven or eight years old, I remember peddling *Liberty Magazine* from door to door. Later I sold the Sunday edition of the *Los Angeles Examiner* newspaper. I can't imagine why anybody in Albuquerque, New Mexico, would have wanted to buy the *Los Angeles Examiner*. But, as with *Liberty Magazine*, there were a few kind souls who donated to charity by buying from me—neighbors and relatives mostly. I especially remember my Uncle Henry, who was filled with generosity when this ragamuffin would walk through the door of the bar he tended downtown. In addition to buying whatever I was selling that week, he would often treat me to a Coke.

In Los Angeles when I was a bit older, Saturdays were days of opportunity. One of my friends and I would turn the lawnmower upside down, hook the grass catcher over the handle, and take turns pushing it along the sidewalk looking for prospects. The other would carry the edger and the broom for sweeping up afterwards. Twenty-five cents was the going rate. We'd sweat and push the dull-edged machine through crab grass that was tough as copper wire and watch anxiously as the neighbor surveyed our efforts and pointed out flaws to be remedied. Then, when we were finally finished, we would walk off tired but exhilarated with our earnings.

One summer I hand set pins in a bowling alley at ten cents a line plus tips. League nights were the bonanzas. If you got to set for leagues, you handled two alleys at a time—twice the money—and the tips were better. I liked the money, but the work didn't agree with me. It wasn't the company, although my parents might have objected if they'd known. Many of the other pinsetters were old winos earning their muscatel money. My problem was purely physical: all that bending over and straightening up turned the food in my stomach to mush. I didn't relish developing a case of the permanent trots and decided to move on to better and healthier work.

There had been that ill-fated job at the Los Angeles Coliseum, but ever undaunted, I thought there was still room for me in the newspaper business. I applied and was hired by the *Southwest Wave*, a two-morning-a-week job delivering the local shopper door to door. It required buoyant optimism since there was no salary. Instead, you collected each month from any household that considered the free throwaway worth paying for.

You had to get up at 5 a.m. on schooldays, stuff a two-sided canvas bag with newspapers, hoist it up so you could stick your head through the hole between the two sides. Then off on foot, folding papers as you walked along, tossing them onto the porches of dark little houses where people with any sense were asleep in their warm beds.

My friends Mickey and Ralph, who shared a route, decided it was more than they bargained for. They dumped their newspapers in the gutter of the nearest street corner and went back home to bed. I plugged on, accompanied by a large mutt of a dog who thought I looked harmless enough and who padded along sniffing trees and hedges and growling at stray cats. A few mornings I would see a dapper little man dressed in a sport coat, slacks, and a fedora taking an early morning constitutional.

My dog companion growled a warning that first morning as I stumbled along half asleep. I looked up to see the little man just ahead. Then a tremendous explosion startled me completely awake. It was followed by a series of lesser eruptions. I didn't understand how so much gas could escape with such violent noise from such a little man—he was no bigger than me! Then he turned the corner leaving me to follow this rancid trail with my dog friend sniffing along beside me. Right then I nicknamed him the Little Pooter, figuring that his wife must have kicked him out of bed—for good reason!

The end of the month made those early morning hours worthwhile. After dinner I'd get out a pencil and pad of receipts, then head for my paper route. I'd knock on the door and mumble, "Collecting for the *Southwest Wave*" in a tone of voice that implied with a touch of hope, "You don't want to pay for this, do you?" Luckily for me, many of the customers did. Ten cents. All of which I got to keep for myself.

I'd head home after an evening of collections—it normally took two or three nights to finish the entire route—my pockets full of dimes. I'd burst into the house, plant myself in the center of the living room, while my parents watched with pleasure and wonder as their budding Rockefeller dumped his dimes on the rug and counted them. I earned twenty dollars that first month. It was enough to keep me going for many more months.

But the summer I finished the eleventh grade I thought it was time for a grown-up job. I had turned fifteen the month before school ended. I intended to tell prospective employers that I was sixteen, since that was the legal age for getting a regular job. If you wanted to work in a defense plant, you had to show your birth certificate to prove it.

I scanned the classified ads and finally found something worth pursuing. "Bright, alert apprentice wanted for summer work in jewelry trades." I took the streetcar to the Jewelry Trades Building in downtown Los Angeles and rode the elevator to the sixth floor. It was a small shop that made custom wristwatch crystals and refinished watch dials, serving jewelers who sent customers' watches for repair.

I walked in brashly and went up to the man behind the counter, Jerry, the foreman. "I understand you want a bright, alert apprentice this summer," I said. "Here I am."

He didn't laugh, but I'm sure he smiled. "How old are you?" he asked. "Sixteen!"

As luck would have it, Jerry was a little fellow. I was about five feet five inches tall at the time, and Jerry was all of five feet three on tiptoes. He must have believed me, and after a brief interview, he hired me. I'm sure it wasn't because of any qualifications for the job—I had none. It might have been my naive, brash manner. Or it may have been that help of any kind was hard to find during the war.

The job paid fifty cents an hour, twenty dollars for a forty-hour week, and I had to join the jewelry trades union. My addition brought the staff up to six people, one woman and five males who, for one reason or another, were not eligible to be in uniform.

In addition to Jerry there was Stella, a woman in her mid-thirties who liked to tease the crippled man whose name I have forgotten and whose wife was pregnant. She would needle him about becoming a father and toss out comments like, "She does all the work while you have all the fun." Or, "Don't get fresh with me. A woman can run faster with her dress off than a man can with his pants down."

There was a tall, lugubrious man in his forties who came dressed in a shirt and tie and looked more like an accountant or a mortician than a jewelry technician. And there was George, a tall, blonde young man of nineteen who had a heart murmur.

I listened to all the banter back and forth while learning how to do the least-skilled parts of shaping and fitting glass of various colors over the faces and dials of wristwatches.

Every day at noon Jerry's girlfriend would come by from another office in the building to pick him up. She was tinier than he, and the two of them, dressed to the nines, would sashay out to lunch like two little walking dolls. I would sit in the shop with my brown-bag baloney sandwich and talk with George, who liked to brag about his women. We'd sit by the inside window that looked across the empty space in the center of the building to the windows on the other side.

One day a large, overweight young woman in a white manicurist's smock waved coyly from a window across the way. "See her?" George said. "I fucked her."

I took a hard look at the smiling young harlot. "Big deal!" I thought.

So passed the months from mid-June to early September. Before I left, I fashioned a blue-tinted watch crystal with beveled edges for my inexpensive wristwatch, no charge from the shop. I promised to come back in the fall and show them my ROTC uniform, and I did.

18

The last year of high school was a flurry of activity. Many of my friends were making plans to join the armed forces after graduation while I only got to play soldier in the ROTC. That first semester I tried out for the glee club—and failed. I couldn't carry a tune in a basket. I worked part-time after school as a page at the local library, shelving books. In uniform with other ROTC members I served as an usher during Saturday afternoon youth concerts at the Philharmonic Auditorium downtown. And of course, there were always classes and homework.

Toward the end of the first semester there was campaigning for positions of leadership on the student body cabinet. I was by then a second lieutenant in the ROTC and a candidate, along with two other second lieutenants, to become commander of the unit the final semester of our senior year.

I lusted for that position of leadership; the ROTC commander was automatically a member of the student body cabinet. But my chances of ending up there were seriously in doubt. Captain Nagelman's obvious favorite was another student, a hard-charging, sharp-shooting, hell-raising young man who could unquestioningly lead a charge over the hill into enemy fire. One of his favorite pastimes was to drive in the desert at night with friends and shoot jackrabbits blinded by the lights of their moving pickup truck using a .22 caliber rifle. He was the best shot on the ROTC rifle team. Many months after graduation he would come back home after combat duty overseas, a badly shaken young man who had been so affected by what he had seen that for a time he studied for the ministry.

I was Sergeant Backell's choice. He was on campus every day, dealing with faculty and administration and had his finger on the pulse of school politics. He was also sensitive to school traditions. For whatever the reason, the student commander of the ROTC unit had almost always been a scholar.

The indecision was frustrating. I decided to fight fire with fire by declaring my candidacy for another student body office, president of the Scholarship Society. Fish or cut bait, I thought, regarding the ROTC position. The major opposition for the Scholarship Society presidency was a girl who would go on to law school and later become the administrative aide for U.S. Senator William Knowland. In these days of more enlightened attitudes, she might have become a senator herself, and a good one.

Prior to the student election the ROTC instructors finally came to a decision. I was selected as cadet lieutenant colonel, commander of the unit, and I withdrew my candidacy for Scholarship Society president.

A subsequent incident put a damper on that happy event. The most prestigious school service club for boys was the Knights. There was an equivalent organization for girls. The Knights consisted of student leaders including athletes, and its sponsor was the teacher who was the faculty adviser for the student body cabinet. Becoming a Knight was the aspiration of most active students because it represented social as well as academic recognition.

I filled out my application. On my way to turn it in, I met a fellow student who had become a member the previous semester. He was one of the social elite of our class and, I thought, something of a snob. I told him what I was about to do. He was eager and in fact insistent on taking care of my application for me. This seemed surprisingly generous, and I gave it to him with high hopes.

A week or two later the names of new members of the Knights were released. My name was not on the list. I was crestfallen. At least when the glee club had not accepted me I knew it was because I had a terrible voice. I didn't understand what happened. I felt snubbed, then decided there must be something lacking in me. After the first bitter disappointment I put it out of my mind and carried on.

Then one day after a student body cabinet meeting, the faculty adviser who was also the teacher-sponsor of the Knights asked to me to stay a moment. "Why didn't you apply to become a Knight?" he asked me.

I was shocked and confused. I explained that I *had* applied, that I had given my application to so-and-so. I don't remember what, if anything, the teacher said. But I was one of two boys on the student body cabinet who had *not* been accepted as a Knight. The other was the head of Boys' Cooperative Government, Norman Shapiro.

Had my classmate lost my application? Deliberately thrown it away? If so, why? Was it personal—that is, for some reason he didn't like me? Was it a case of youthful carelessness? Or was it out-and-out prejudice?

One of the students who had been accepted as a Knight was the boys' vice president, a popular student and athlete who happened to be black. A girl member of the student body cabinet was accepted into the girls' equivalent service organization. She, like Norman, was Jewish.

I never confronted my erring classmate who lost my application. I was rather shy and uncertain about such matters. Being younger than most of my classmates, I was socially backward and unassertive. I don't remember if he ever apologized to me. My recollection is that he did not.

But life goes on. Just ahead I was to confront something more important to my then-unknown aspirations to be a writer: my first professional writing job.

19

The second half of our senior year was busier than ever. There were responsibilities for running the ROTC battalion, duties as a student body officer, social activities, and studies. I found that I couldn't handle it all and still work twenty hours a week, so I quit my job at the public library. I was on the dole again.

A group of us, including my friend Phil Mannion, would walk home together after school. Occasionally we would stop at the malt shop and have one of those high-calorie ice-cream concoctions. I could afford this once in a while, but it soon developed into an everyday event.

At the same time there was some activity at school for which I was collecting money—money that I wouldn't have to turn in for a few weeks. You could see what was going to happen. Belly up to the bar, boys! How about a chocolate caramel sundae with walnuts and whipped cream, topped by a maraschino cherry? Heedless, a slave to my sweet tooth as well as not wanting to admit to my friends that I had no money, I borrowed from this fund that I was collecting—without, unfortunately, considering where I would get the money to pay it back.

Some semblance of sense finally prevailed after a couple of weeks, probably because the deadline for turning in the funds was looming. I tallied up my records (after all, I usually got A's in math) and found that I was four dollars short. It might as well have been forty or four hundred. The going wage was fifty cents an hour, if you had a job. There was no way that I could ask my parents for money. Things were always tight at home, and they would have been hard put to spare four dollars, even if they had been sympathetic. Embezzlement stared me in the face. I was in a jam.

I wandered around school with this dark cloud hovering over me, threatening a deluge. What would the teacher who was the sponsor for the activity think when I came up short four dollars? What would fellow students think? What about my reputation for honor? For integrity?

Wallowing in this sinkhole of despair, I made my way past the auto shop one day. "Psst!" came a whispered call. It was the stereotypic beckoning of a shady character on a street corner enticing you to buy some ill-gotten goods at an unbelievably low price.

There, leaning against the corner of the entrance to the auto shop was the alleged student kingpin of high school gamblers. When he showed up in school at all, he wandered the halls with a copy of the racing form in his hip pocket. He had entree to the tracks at Santa Anita and Hollywood Park, preferring the ponies to *The Mill on the Floss* in English class. Dice and decks of playing cards were his obedient servants.

We did not travel in the same circles, but we knew each other by reputation. "Listen," he said when I went over. "How'd you like to make five bucks?"

Manna from heaven! Maybe he was going to give me a tip on a sure thing in the third race—if I could raise two dollars and place a bet. I was not unfamiliar with the ponies. My father was one of those hopeful two-dollar bettors who spent his life waiting for his long shot to come in, in the meantime enriching the local bookie whose barbershop was probably only a front.

"Sure," I said.

"I need a report," he said. "By the end of the week." He said that he was about to flunk English if he didn't turn in this project.

On my way home after school I stopped at the library instead of the malt shop. Although I don't remember the subject of the report, I remember that I dug into it with a zeal even greater than trying to get the top grade in class. I researched the bejesus out of it. Not only that afternoon, but also that evening after dinner when I returned to the library. The next night or two my portable typewriter with the capped keys hummed, blind to the fingers hard at work ghostwriting.

The gambler and I kept our rendezvous at the appointed time. He folded the report lengthwise and slipped it into the inside pocket of his loafer jacket. Then he slipped me the fiver. Saved! I turned in the funds that I'd collected before temptation should once more raise its siren voice, and I vowed to stay away from the malt shop forever. I could live again, my nefarious behavior a secret.

A week or so later as I was walking down the hall of one of the buildings, the faculty adviser for the Scholarship Society called to me. I was an active member of the group and assumed that it had something to do with a forthcoming meeting.

There was fire in her eyes. "Young man—," she began. I knew it was something serious. When she started to talk about the ethics of writing a report for another student, it came to me. *She* was the gambler's English teacher. I had been in her English class the year before, and she knew me from the Scholarship Society. There was no way she was going to believe that the gambler had written that report. And under pressure, he had squealed.

She was really angry. "Integrity, young man!" was her parting shot. "Integrity!"

Later that day I got a summons to the boys' vice principal's office. Was he going to expel me? I could see the headline splashed across the school newspaper: "ROTC Commander Expelled for Fraud!"

In summation, the vice principal said that he was sure that I did it out of friendship, not for any monetary gain. But never do it again. I kept my mouth shut and my eyes downcast.

When the gambler and I saw each other again we shared mutual commiseration. He said to keep the five dollars as conscience money for his finking on me. (I had no intention of giving it back.) From his point of view he had bet five dollars on a horse that had won the race but had been disqualified.

I learned that there is no free ice-cream soda. And I also learned that you can get paid for writing words, something that would come back to me years later.

20

In addition to school and work, of course, there was home and church. It was at this time that my parents were having the rockiest period in their marriage. Perhaps being a teenager trying to become independent and grown-up made me highly sensitive to what was going on. Although I do remember a time before when I was about eleven years old and my parents had a terrible row. It ended with my father slapping my mother. I was both frightened and angry. I thrust myself between them and started punching at him. "Don't you hit my mother!" I shouted.

It was the only instance that I remember of my father hitting my mother. He was not a physically violent man, but he could get angry and shout in a loud voice that was very intimidating. I remember receiving very few spankings growing up. It wasn't that I was that well behaved; I had a mouth.

The slap was no doubt a sign of the attitudes of the times. There was Jimmy Cagney in the movies pushing a grapefruit in Mae Clark's face. There were many movies of the era where the male character would slap, spank, or otherwise manhandle his lady. It seemed acceptable. Father may or may not have known best, but in those times he ruled the roost—by force if necessary.

I never knew what my parents' quarrels were about—probably money. Or how to raise children. Or my mother's independence. I always felt that she was the one who pushed out into the broader world, moving away from the farm and beyond the old closed-society Hispanic attitudes that my father could never completely shake.

In that culture the father's word was final. He brooked no argument. I can remember seeing men of fifty or sixty years of age quake before their feeble, angry, despotic old fathers who were laying down the law.

My father got more than he bargained for when he married a flapper. Right off the bat she refused his brothers' offer to build them a house on family property in the country next door to one or the other of the relatives. She felt her in-laws were meddlesome enough without living next door to them. She shocked her sisters-in-law by learning to drive a car—women weren't supposed to drive cars back then. And horrors! She would drive her young children across town to visit their Rivera grandmother—*without another woman as a chaperone.* Worse yet, she smoked cigarettes. The hussy!

Certainly another factor in her independence was my father's job. He would be gone on the train for several days at a time, and while he was gone, mother was in charge. She was used to taking things into her own hands and doing what was necessary, while my father could be hapless at times. She was not timid about dealing with trades people, whereas my father often retreated from such. One family incident that they laughed about took place when I was quite small, perhaps about three years old. A bill collector knocked on the door, and my father hid in the closet to avoid him. When mother opened the front door, I ran to the closet and rattled the doorknob, pointing and shouting, "Daddy! Daddy!" The bill collector left with a look of suspicion on his face, promising to be back when the mister was home.

But it was during my junior year in high school that things really came to a head with my parents. My sister and I were not innocent bystanders. We had our own quarrels with our father, who, in addition to whatever other problems he had, did not know how to cope with growing teenagers pushing for independence. "Leave him!" we said to mother. "Divorce him! He's being awful!"

This was serious stuff. Divorce was not taken lightly in those days. Especially among Catholics. My sister and I were too young to understand the economic dependence involved. Our mother had been a housewife during her marriage; it would only be later that she would go out to work.

In spite of this, Mother asked Father for a divorce. He was shocked. He saw that she was really serious. She finally got his attention. In alarm, he called on the pastor of our church for help. I can remember the night that Father Dee came to call. He was a stout, sandy-haired man whom I remember rolling along the aisles of the church during Friday night stations of the cross during Lent as if on sea legs not yet used to flat earth. You could see the glaze on his face and smell the wine that he had liberally helped himself to before services.

That evening visit was not a consultation or even much of a discussion. Even at my young age I could see it for what it was: a male chauvinist Catholic power play. Divorce was a sin! A wife should be obedient to her husband! Not a word that I remember was about verbal abuse, about their problems that needed discussion, about my mother's point of view. I felt that my father's pandering to the pastor was weak and inexcusable, especially since Father only went to church occasionally, when it suited him. It was my mother who was the devout Catholic and who remained one all of her life in spite of idiots like Father Dee.

The parting words of wisdom from the priest to my mother were, "Take off your bobby socks. You're a grown woman." Incredible.

When the pastor, left he took not a little of my Catholicism with him. What kind of a man was this to speak for God? My father sensed the still unsettled state of affairs and made his final plea. He would sign over the house to her. Not a word about changing his behavior. But he was a frightened and chastened man, being brought this close to the brink with his troublesome wife defiant even to the priest.

I don't know what conversations they had in private. I never knew what my mother moiled over before coming to a final decision. I do know that she didn't divorce him. There must have been many considerations, such as the sixteen years she had invested in a marriage and her fervent Catholicism that remained steadfast even after dealing with an insensitive lout of a priest. (There was no question in my mind that she was more a child of God than this representative of the clergy.) She probably weighed the prospect of going to work to support herself and, if the children had anything to say about it, two growing children who would soon be on their own. I'm certain it wasn't the house that father offered to sign over to her; she was not a person to be bribed. She had a stiff and stubborn pride. And as far as I know, the house never was signed over to her.

Their sometimes turbulent marriage was not without its effects on my sister and me. I acknowledge having become cautious. At a time when many of my friends married immediately after graduating from college, it took me seven years to finally come around. My sister, after four marriages—one annulment (to remain a Catholic) and three divorces—finished her life as a single woman.

As for mother, for whatever reasons, she decided to stick it out. Thirty-seven years later, when she had been a widow for a few years, she confided to me how lonely she was. How much she missed my father. Somewhere along the way they had made their peace.

21

As the end of the high school senior year drew near, the main topic of concern for most young men was the military, whereas it was college for some of the young women and a few underage boys like me. Some, like my friend Dave Wright, had already been drafted into service. Others, like my friend Phil Mannion, had volunteered for Naval Air Corps gunners' school and would be leaving for training a short time after graduation.

Becoming a writer was the farthest thing from my mind. I had always been a great reader for pleasure, but it was just that: fun, escape. It never occurred to me that real people wrote the books I enjoyed so much. None of my relatives or my parents' friends were writers or even teachers. They were just regular people. Carpenters. House painters. Waiters. Short-order cooks. Barbers. Gardeners. Housewives. Almost all of the women were housewives. The closest thing to an artist of any sort might have been my father's cousin Sam García, who had a rumba band that played clubs in East L.A. Or my Uncle Herminio Chávez, who had once been with a group that sang on the radio in Albuquerque. The best jobs of all were with the government, civil service, which were guaranteed for life even though they didn't pay as much as other jobs. Security—that was the big thing if you came to adulthood during the Depression, as my father did.

There was no question in my mind that college was the next step. Teachers had always been encouraging. In looking back I realize how much I owe to so many. They pointed the way. They held me up to standards. They opened my eyes to worlds I never dreamed of.

My parents believed in education and were positive about college. My father had gone to Las Vegas Normal School, now New Mexico Highlands

University, in Las Vegas, New Mexico, for a year. He had planned to be a schoolteacher but found that it was not for him.

But where to go? Where to apply? My first choice was the University of Southern California. No doubt because they had such terrific football teams, and the campus was nearby. The problem was that the tuition at USC was too expensive.

Like some of my schoolmates in ROTC, I thought about trying for an appointment to West Point. In spite of my patriotic fervor, becoming a professional soldier didn't really appeal to me, even if there had been the likelihood of getting an appointment. Anyway, how did you go about such things? I hadn't the faintest idea.

I never seriously considered Los Angeles City College, although a number of my friends did. I applied instead to the nearest campus of the state university, the University of California, Los Angeles. It was academically challenging—only the top ten percent of high school graduates were eligible to apply. It had a fine reputation even though it stood in the shadow of its big brother campus at Berkeley. And it was affordable—almost.

Fine. That was settled. But go to college for what? That was the dilemma. What was I going to do with my life? What did a kid who turned sixteen a month before high school graduation know about his possible life's work? What did I know about anything?

One of the most exacting measures of a high school student's ability was how well he or she did in science and math. Only the brains managed to get good grades in courses like chemistry and physics—or even to pass them. These subjects challenged the most competitive students to their fiercest efforts, and it was by doing well in these subjects that student reputations were made. In science and math there were real right and wrong answers to questions, not the ambiguity of essay questions as in English or history. All of the students entered class with the same lack of background—few of the students' parents were scientists or engineers at that time. The great explosion in science and scientists was to come later, as a result of World War II. There were no cultural disadvantages as in social studies, where your family might not subscribe to *Time* magazine.

I don't know if the idea came from my parents or from me—I had done well in science and math—but suddenly there was talk of becoming a doctor. It sounded grand and glorious. "My son, the doctor." But it was tinged with naïveté. Why do so many doctors' sons (and now daughters) become doctors? They know something about the business, including what it costs in time, dedication, and money to get educated. And they can afford it! There was no such consideration in our family. What did I know about being a doctor? Did I really want to be one? Money was one of three important things our parents never discussed with us. The others were sex and ethnicity.

Somehow, though, it happened. Suddenly I was going to go to college to become a doctor. If someone asked what I was going to study in college, I'd say to be a doctor. I would enter UCLA as a premedical major. Then there came more practical considerations—like money. This failed ghostwriter would have to depend on his parents' inadequate finances. My mother, God bless her, volunteered to go to work.

Prior to these times very few married women worked outside of the home. It took the absence of men in the military, plus the enormous productive requirements for winning the war, to give women their chance. It was the time of Rosie the Riveter—women who took all kinds of jobs that only men did before, including work on production lines in defense plants.

My mother went to work on the production line of a subcontractor to a major aircraft plant. They produced metal honeycomb core that went into the wings of airplanes.

While all this was going on, there was still high school. I was not part of the social circuit. I was quadruple-cursed: too young, no money, no car, and shy. Still, there were some must-do events. The ROTC ball. The senior prom. A class beach party on a night that grunion were supposed to run. I never saw a grunion.

I had no regular girlfriend, so I had acute teenage angst in getting up the courage to ask someone, only to find out I had waited too long and she already had a date, and then to ask someone else.

Graduation night I remember vaguely. The boys and many of the girls went out stag. In Los Angeles, there was no more exciting place you could go to stay up all night than Hollywood! It was pretty innocent by any standard. We didn't drink liquor and definitely didn't do drugs. I don't think any of us knew anything about drugs except that jazz musicians smoked marijuana and some of us listened to jazz records.

I can remember one fellow a year ahead of us who had been a classical pianist while in high school. He moved to Seattle—apparently he was not eligible for the draft—and made a living playing jazz. I saw him on the street-car in our neighborhood one day in drape pants and porkpie hat (he was not Chicano or black), his eyes puffy and red, standing wobbly while hanging onto a leather strap, stoned out of his mind. But that was rare in those days.

As I remember, the big-deal graduation night involved going to an Italian restaurant in Hollywood dressed up in our best clothes. Years later I would see a photograph taken that night and be moved by the eclectic make-up of that all-American crew, the youthful, unself-conscious tolerance and cama-raderie. We were friends having a good time together.

Later that night we met some girls from our graduating class, stag like us. We joined up and continued the evening. I don't remember what we did. We probably went for a cup of coffee in some all-night drive-in so we could stay awake. We greeted the dawn, then parted to drive our separate, sleepy ways home.

On June 11, 1994, the Manual Arts High School graduating class of 1944 held its fifty-year reunion at the Radisson Hotel in Irvine, California. It was attended by almost 200 people—graduates and spouses alike. Among the signs of the times was the locale of the reunion. The Radisson Hotel is in suburban Orange County adjacent to the John Wayne Airport. It is near affluent coastal cities approximately forty miles south of Manual Arts High School, which is located in South Central Los Angeles, scene of the 1992 riots. Sometimes cities—and neighborhoods—change even more than old alumni. Gray hair and wrinkles are, after all, superficial, while the core person, though perhaps mellowed or sometimes embittered by age, remains essentially the same.

This was a group that was born in the late 1920s and grew up during the Depression. They appeared to be comfortably well-off. Retired for the most part. Mostly in good health. Not just parents, but grandparents and not an insignificant number of great-grandparents.

There was a brief ceremony before dinner. The flag salute led by the high school ROTC commander seemed appropriate for this World War II class. We had entered high school three months before Pearl Harbor and gradu-ated two weeks after D-Day. An invocation by a Catholic deacon reflected the changes in that not-quite-monolithic religion.

After dinner there was a brief program. There was the singing of school songs and presentation of awards, among them the farthest traveled (Connecticut), longest married (three couples for fifty years), most grand-children (twenty-one). Then, in memoriam, names were read of forty-one deceased classmates of the more than 500 graduates. A gray-haired old friend of Chinese ancestry leaned on his cane as he told me about one of the deceased. He had been a navy photographer stationed on board an aircraft carrier during the war. A bomb landed on deck, destroying his workstation.

A number of letters were read from classmates who were unable to attend. One poignant letter, from a woman of Japanese ancestry, recalled that she had been unable to take part in her high school graduation and was sorry to miss this reunion. She and her family had spent the war in an internment camp, having lost nearly everything they had owned including remembrances of her high school years.

After the program there was the benediction by a minister classmate. Then began the music and dancing and visiting. It was a nostalgic evening with more energy spent renewing old friendships than dancing either slow or jitterbug to the disk-jockeyed records of the period: Glenn Miller, Artie Shaw, Johnny Mercer, Jo Stafford, and others.

It was a wonderful get-together—a memorable experience. As if in a time warp, the years dropped away and friendships were renewed as if we had seen each other just last week.

One of the graduates had converted old home movies of the period to videocassette. The scenes of campus life and graduation showed young people full of hope, energy, fun, and goodwill even in wartime. But the most moving were the scenes of students seeing fellow graduates off at the train station on their way to navy boot camp. These young men had enlisted in an aerial gunners' program and were setting off on important adult business. Kids eighteen years old doing what had to be done.

Graduation time was, in retrospect, a coming-of-age when we were united in something bigger than ourselves. No divisiveness of ethnic groups—many graduates had married outside of their own group. No readiness to point fingers at each other. Perhaps the presence of a common enemy united us, just as now without such obvious devils we tend to look among ourselves for someone to blame. Or perhaps in our innocence we did not yet see those things beneath the surface that needed to be changed.

The times then seemed warmer and more accepting in the light of all that is happening today. And in coming together after fifty years, it seemed that when our lives first touched, it was an embrace that warmed our memories forever.

22

UCLA was on a wartime footing when I enrolled in July 1944. Three full semesters were crammed into the school year although many students only attended two of the three semesters. As I recall, there were something like 4,000 to 4,500 students on campus that first semester, a far cry from the teeming campus of today.

In addition to the young women on campus, there was also a contingent of young, uniformed men, participants in the Navy V-12 College Training Program. These were sailors going to college at government expense for special training before being sent off to war. Then there were the 4-F's, ineligible for military service for physical or mental reasons, and the underage young men like myself. As the lyrics of a popular wartime song, always sung by a female singer, went:

> They're either too young or too old.
> They're either too gray or too grassy green.
> The pickings are poor and the crop is lean.
> What's good is in the Army.
> What's left will never harm me.

The campus, which was in Westwood, was about fifteen miles from home. It took between an hour and an hour and fifteen minutes by bus, with one transfer at Wilshire Boulevard. Eight a.m. classes were hell. It meant catching a bus no later than six-thirty. The theory was that you could study during the long commute. Forget it! The swaying, rocking bus was more conducive to sleep. And timing was important. If you missed a bus connection, there was a wait that meant you'd be late for class.

I was an average student in college. Actually my so-so performance started during my senior year of high school. I suddenly became aware that there was more to the world than school. A certain lethargy and independence had set in, something that my classmates had probably gone through earlier. Being younger, I had some catching up to do, including that bid for independence that in its most extreme would be rebellion. With me it was more a matter of sluffing off in school and daydreaming, plus arguing with my father about what I considered his stupid, old-fashioned ideas.

Those freshman semesters at UCLA I did get A's in chemistry and military science. (Since UCLA was a land grant college, ROTC was required in the freshman and sophomore years in addition to regular physical education.) But German was my downfall. A friend and I were the class dummkopfs. We passed by the grace of God and the kindness of our professor, Herr Melnitz. Professor Melnitz was a refugee from Austria, which had been overrun by the Nazis. He had been in the theatre in his native country, and he later taught in and became head of the UCLA Theatre Arts Department. He was a much beloved and talented man for whom Melnitz Hall was named.

I can still see his eyebrows rise dramatically as we walked into class after cutting a session—or two or maybe even three. His Germanic accent flooded the room as the other students turned to watch us enter. "Ah. Herr Candelaria. Herr Levine. So nice of you to join us."

We slunk to our seats with chagrin and opened our little green text, *Einer Kleiner Garten*, or the book about Leo Slezak, the opera singer, who was the father of the Hollywood actor Walter Slezak. We steeled ourselves to be called on for a translation and thus be shamed once again for our ineptitude.

I never understood why I resisted the language. I had suffered through Latin in junior high and high school and had done well enough. And Herr Melnitz was my favorite professor by far. He was a jolly, warm human being who tolerated his class dummkopfs with not a little indulgence and amusement.

But there was something about German. It had nothing to do with being at war with the country. The connection between learning the language in a classroom and the Nazis was extremely remote. Perhaps it was because German was *the* required language for science majors, which included pre-medical students. I was stretching my independence at the time, and my general attitude was that if I liked the subject, I'd work hard and do well. If it bored me, I would slide through with as little effort as possible. Sliding through German required more effort than most classes.

After those first two semesters, other students from our high school enrolled at UCLA. One of them, another underage young man like myself, had a car. It was a time when very few young people owned automobiles. I'm sure there had been less than half a dozen cars owned by students in my high school senior class of 500. Because of the war, new cars were not being manufactured for civilian use. Everyone made do with the old jalopy they had owned before the war broke out.

In addition, gasoline was rationed. Carpooling was common. People pulled together to support the war effort. Sharing cars was patriotic. So six of us crammed into Bob Bloch's bright blue Chevrolet sedan that was at least ten years old. We chipped in our bus money to keep that old car running. I don't recall if we contributed gasoline ration stamps to the kitty. It may be that Bob received an extra allotment of stamps because of the car pool. Or maybe there were enough stamps to eke out the trips to and from campus.

It was a jolly crew that varied from time to time, depending on the schedules of the individual passengers: a few young men still too young to be drafted and several young women. A ride to make an eight a.m. class was absolutely essential. Those whose going-home schedules were not the same as Bob's took the bus.

It could be a long day sometimes, with breaks in the student union over coffee, or dealing out a deck of playing cards to try to learn how to play bridge, or sitting on the lawn under the shade of a tree and watching the world (and the girls) go by.

In between, of course, there would be classes. And even occasional study in the huge library. It was so much more grown-up than high school, and we relished our newfound freedom and the intellectual climate that surrounded us but that we didn't always take advantage of. The standing joke was that some of us were majoring in bridge rather than academics. What amazes me in retrospect was that even in the midst of the world's turmoil, young people could still find joy in simple pleasures, as if the war overseas was a bad dream.

23

One of the interesting differences from high school was that ROTC was compulsory for male freshmen and sophomores and was taken in addition to, rather than instead of, physical education. Because of my high school ROTC training, I was made a cadet officer that first semester at UCLA. Almost none of the other cadets had previous ROTC experience. I must have been full of self-importance, a pompous little cadet lieutenant. I was my father's son, barking out commands for close order drill with a "Hut! Two! Three! Four!" as if I was pushing a switch and automatons would respond.

What I didn't realize was that the group under my command was not cut from military cloth. They did not cotton to this loud little snip yelling at them. They did not share my naïveté about the importance of it all, coming from more middle-class backgrounds where the military was not a sacred duty. There may even have been a few among them who would have gladly avoided the draft.

Another cadet officer, a tall, wiry student who was on the water polo team (Water polo? What was water polo? Was this like horse polo for the elite who swam?), stopped me and offered some advice. "Go easy on the fellows," he said. "Otherwise they won't like you."

Won't like me! I thought. What did that have to do with anything?

I found out the next week in drill. The platoon was marching along at the proper military cadence, Springfield rifles at right shoulder arms. I barked out the command, "To the rear. . . march!" The platoon responded all right—in four different directions with a few cadets standing in the center of this mess marking time.

"There go my people," I might have thought. "I must follow them. For I am their leader."

Instead I reacted in a way totally unexpected by the cadets in the platoon. I started to laugh. I couldn't help it. The whole thing was so damned ridiculous. It had been choreographed like the Keystone Cops hunting for a burglar. Or multiple clones of Laurel and Hardy destroying something they were trying to construct.

Through the laughter I shouted, "Platoon, halt!" And they did. But it was my laughter that saved the situation. When they turned toward me, expecting, I suppose, to see me apoplectic, they too started to laugh. And after a few minutes we reassembled, trying to control our sense of the ludicrous. After that I tempered my marine sergeant's bellow to a less demanding shout. And though I still issued the same commands, they seemed to be taken with more grace. I don't know if the fellows liked me or not, but we got along.

The next summer the importance of ROTC diminished. One of the grandest birthday gifts I ever received was on May 7, 1945, my seventeenth birthday. That was the day the German surrender was signed. The next day it was announced to the world. VE Day! The war in Europe was over.

Right after that I entered the final semester of compulsory ROTC. I had a good relationship with Colonel Barker, our professor of military science and tactics. A short, gray-haired man of slight build, he was regular army, probably in his sixties, and therefore a bit old for combat duty. I never knew what his military experience had been. But I do remember his telling us how you could combat thirst when water rations were low. You put a pebble in your mouth, under your tongue, and the saliva generated helped you forget your need for water. Somehow I had the picture of him as a young lieutenant out in the desert with General Pershing's troops, a pebble under his tongue, chasing Pancho Villa. He would have been about the right age.

Colonel Barker was a soft-spoken, friendly man who approved of my zeal for ROTC, unlike many of my fellow cadets. It was about this time that I first tried out for the track team, and I can remember him walking leisurely out to the bleachers in full uniform to watch the team work out.

It must have been after one such workout that he spoke to me about continuing with ROTC in my junior and senior years. There were advantages. First of all, they paid you a stipend to finish college, and money was always a concern for me. After graduation you were commissioned a second lieutenant and entered active duty for a period of two years before returning to civilian life and a position as an officer in the army reserve.

Germany had just surrendered. It would not be long before the Japanese would follow. My military zeal had been slowly eroding, and I was nearing the completion of my premedical requirements so I would be able to apply for medical school the next year. I was flattered by his recruiting offer, but I politely declined.

24

There was heightened excitement about the war after the Germans surrendered. I can remember rumors floating around the Chemistry Department about mysterious, secret research going on that would shorten the war with the Japanese. There had also been a sigh of relief because now that Germany had surrendered, we need not fear the power of *their* research, reputedly some of the best in the world. Nowhere, though, did I hear whispers about what was going on in Los Alamos, New Mexico.

For me there was still the mundane. Attending school all year allowed me to enter my junior year in the fall of 1945. To my schedule of commuting, classes, and study, I added a part-time job. Because I did well in my courses, I was able to hire out as a tutor for freshman chemistry, which paid considerably more than the fifty-cents-an-hour minimum wage of the time.

Later, since I had completed a course in quantitative chemical analysis and done well, I landed a better part-time job. One of my fellow students, a very bright young man named Arnold Miller, had been working for Professor William Crowell, who headed the quantitative analysis curriculum in the Chemistry Department. Arnold needed an assistant and asked if I'd be interested.

As laboratory assistants, we made up samples for analysis by students enrolled in Professor Crowell's quantitative analysis classes. We also helped grade test papers. It was an ideal job for a student. There were no set hours. We could work anytime we wanted, including weekends, as long as we got the job done per schedule. And we could put in as many hours a week as we wanted; there was always plenty of work. Since the pay was decent, it was almost like having a bank account we could draw on.

While I didn't know it at the time—I was still completing required courses so I could apply for medical school—what I learned on this job eventually was to lead to my career in science and scientific writing.

Professor Crowell was an old-school analytical chemist who would retire before I graduated in 1948. Somewhere along the way he had studied in Germany. In the early part of the twentieth century German science, including chemistry, was reputed as the most advanced in the world. German was the international language of chemistry, my experiences with Professor Melnitz notwithstanding. Professor Crowell, a somewhat stiff, old-fashioned man in my eyes, would sometimes deign to talk to us lowly undergraduates about his experiences in Europe, where his wife had studied bel canto. But beneath that reserved and formal nature was a kindly man who looked after his boys.

Analytical chemistry at that time was a crude, test-tube science. One dealt with filtered precipitates and measured volumes of solution delivered by pipets into clean flasks. It depended upon delicate balances for weighing minute quantities of solid material. Calibrated burets were used to titrate solutions in Erlenmeyer flasks to a point where the color of the solution changed. By reading the volume delivered from the buret to cause this color change, you could determine how much of a given chemical was in the solution. This was how we analyzed what and how much was in a given sample.

Meanwhile, in university and government laboratories throughout the country, a revolution was going on in analytical chemistry, leading to new developments essential to the war effort, such as spectrophotometric instruments to help in the development of synthetic rubber (most of the natural rubber supply in the world had fallen into Japanese hands).

After the war these developments gave rise to the formation of an entirely new industry, the analytical instrument business. It was a business in which I spent most of my working career, first as a technical writer and then in advertising and promotion to scientists, while in spare hours and on weekends I wrote fiction. It was a business whose instruments would later make possible analysis of minute quantities of substances in water, air, and soil—quantities equivalent to a pinch of salt in a normal-size swimming pool—thus helping solve contemporary environmental problems. Some instruments allowed detection of the almost undetectable: drugs and other substances in the body fluids of Olympic athletes as well as traces of substances used as evidence in convicting drug dealers. But back during World War II, it was test tubes and flasks and balances.

In retrospect, Professor Crowell was a tolerant man. At one time I reduced one of his laboratories to shambles in the course of washing dozens of large bottles that were to contain unknown solutions for students to analyze. After washing and rinsing the bottles with distilled water, I carefully placed them upside down on layers of paper towels on the tops of long laboratory benches. During the course of the work, I somehow—I'll never know how—tipped a bottle at the end of one of the benches. I was horrified as I stood, helpless, watching the domino effect on glass bottles. Each one in that long, long row knocked into its neighbor, toppled onto the wooden bench, then onto the cement floor. The crash brought people running into the laboratory from that entire end of the chemistry building as I stood in the wreckage of what had once been an intact laboratory.

I apologized to Professor Crowell for my grievous sin. I offered to pay for the bottles, but he would have none of it. I don't even remember if he admonished me to be more careful in the future. I suspect that he knew I had learned my lesson.

The other offense probably stretched Professor Crowell's tolerance considerably more. He was a very prim and proper man, a gentleman of the old school, the age of our grandfathers.

As the laboratory workload increased, a third undergraduate assistant was added. Ernie had recently been discharged from the army and was one of the earliest veterans returning to college. He enjoyed regaling Arnold and me, still too young to be drafted into the military, with his war stories and an occasional song. We must have been taking a break during our lab work one day when Ernie began to sing one of his ditties. I'm not sure if this one was even strictly an army song. It was "The Dirty Boogie." Arnold and I were laughing in sophomoric idiocy as Ernie sang at the top of his lungs in the large, empty laboratory.

Ernie was reaching a crescendo when I turned and saw, but did not hear, the laboratory door open. Professor Crowell entered, stopped when he heard the din, and stood by the door. The last of the lyrics bellowed forth from Ernie— ". . . yelling nooky for sale!"—when he and Arnold must have seen the expression on my face. They turned, startled, and also saw Professor Crowell.

"Gentlemen," he said, as if passing us on a walk through the park on a fine spring day and tipping his hat. Then he turned and left the lab.

We sheepishly and hurriedly returned to our work. Arnold was upset because he was supposed to be our lead man and keep things under control, but every time he tried to pull rank we ridiculed him almost to tears. Ernie was appropriately upset because he was the perpetrator of the vulgar scene. God! What did Professor Crowell think? Our only hope was that he didn't know the meaning of the word "nooky."

The good Professor never mentioned the matter. He might even have gone back to his office and had a good chuckle. No doubt he had had other sophomoric laboratory scut-work boys, and he didn't hold such stupidities against us. In my senior year he helped me when I experienced difficulty with another professor in the Chemistry Department. After graduation, when I applied for my first job as a chemist, he recommended me to my future boss as being a very assiduous worker. Nary a word about my clumsiness or immaturity.

I can imagine that fine old gentleman, in a double-breasted suit and a tie, hair neatly combed, standing erect in the Valhalla of old-time analytical chemists, his wife (whom I never met) in long ball gown beside him. I envision the two of them holding hands as she sings bel canto something much more refined than "The Dirty Boogie."

25

Those were long but enjoyable days. Up early to arrive on campus for eight o'clock classes. Study or work late into the afternoon or sometimes on into the evening. Then the bus home.

Home was the place I slept and had my laundry done. I saw little of my parents except on the weekends that I didn't work. My sister was finishing high school and would soon follow me to UCLA for a short, one-year academic career.

It was during this time, late 1945 and early 1946, that I finally got involved in something of which my father was genuinely proud (not that he hadn't been pleased with my school accomplishments in the past, but I wasn't exactly Phi Beta Kappa material): I went out for and made the UCLA track team.

It was not one of the great years for UCLA track; those were to come much later. The influx of veterans returning from the military services had not yet inundated the campus. There were only the underage, the infirm, and those young men in the Navy V-12 program from which to recruit a team. Luckily, from a competitive point of view, all the other schools in the Pacific Coast Conference had the same problem.

I had not taken physical education in high school and thus had only an ROTC track meet in my senior year with which to test myself. I had won the 100-yard dash and the broad jump.

I enjoyed sports, except for swimming. I was a nonswimmer and terrified of the water, and never more so than when we had to jump off the high diving platform into the swimming pool to meet one of the physical education class requirements. But I found that running was something I could do. We ran cross-country over the hills south of Westwood Boulevard, which helped get me into some kind of shape after my lack of high school activity.

This was just one of the many events in which we were timed, measured, or evaluated, our grades dependent upon how well we did. Somehow I had the feeling that the regular PE instructors used these tests to scout for the varsity athletic teams, always on the lookout for prospects. It was pretty slim pickings in those days.

In one such time trial, I ran the 100-yard dash in a time that was not bad for tennis shoes and lack of training. The instructor encouraged me to try out for the track team. I might not be fast enough to develop into a first-rate sprinter, he said, but perhaps I could stretch out and run the quarter mile.

The track coach was Harry Trotter, a genial man with a girth that reminded me of the movie actor Sidney Greenstreet. The trainer and co-coach was Elvin "Ducky" Drake, who also had a wonderful way with students. When Harry Trotter retired, Ducky Drake became head track coach and one of the legends of the UCLA athletic department.

Training for track was more challenging than my academic classes. There was the discipline and the pain. The whole point was to *win*, and if you wanted to win you had to be in the best possible shape. My little jaunts over the hills of Westwood hardly qualified me for that.

First there was the alternate jogging and walking to slowly get the legs and lungs in shape. Then, as we rounded into shape, the wind sprints—short bursts at full speed. That was interspersed with the killer regimen for developing stamina: alternately running and walking quarter miles, four each, with the runs timed at under sixty seconds. Then later, when we were in decent shape, we would practice starts from starting blocks and run time trials. As the track season approached, the workouts and time trials became more intense. It was on the basis of the time trials that decisions were made as to who would be competing in the coming meet.

On the day of the meet those who were to compete would trade in their everyday gray sweat suits for the itchy navy blue dress versions with gold letters, their gray flannel shorts and sleeveless shirts for white rayon shorts and shirts with blue and gold letters and piping. We had to compete in style. We even had a training table the night before, where we gorged ourselves on thick steaks in plenty of time to digest before the meet.

As I mentioned before, the pickings were slim during the war years, especially among the sprinters. The team did have good athletes competing in the discus, the quarter mile, the half mile, and especially in the hurdles. Our hurdler was an outstanding athlete who made it to the trials for the 1948 Olympic Games. If he hadn't hit a hurdle and tripped, he would have had an excellent chance of representing the United States that year. As for the sprinters, suffice it to say that we normally entered three runners in the meets, and I managed to be the third entrant in the 100-yard dash fairly often, run the 220-yard dash on occasion, and usually be one of the quartet of runners in the sprint relays.

It was fun. We traveled on the overnight train to compete with Stanford University at Palo Alto, California, and took the bus to San Diego for a relay meet—gas rationing and limited train space notwithstanding. On one occasion I somehow managed to take third in a 100-yard dash, and a photograph of the runners breaking the finish tape was splashed across the sports page of the Los Angeles Times. My Notre Dame sidewalk alumni friends in our church parish couldn't get over it.

It was during this time that my father communicated to me one of the two things I remember that told me he cared. Whenever he'd see a friend or relative while I was with him, he'd manage to brag, "My son was a track star in college when he was eighteen years old." I'd be embarrassed and think, hardly. But for my father, who often bragged how he had once beaten the school's star sprinter in a race when he was at Albuquerque High School, this was a big deal. For years after it was the only accomplishment of mine he ever seemed to remember and comment on.

The other thing he did touched me more. It was a couple of years later, while I was working as a chemist and trying to write short stories. I was living in my parents' home, paying room and board. I'd mail out my stories to various magazines, eternally hopeful that my genius would be discovered. What I received was training in one of the cardinal requirements for a serious creative writer: learning to deal with rejection. The other important requirement is to have an independent income.

The envelopes would come back with printed rejection slips. I can't remember my father ever reading one of my stories. His tastes were more toward the pulp magazines of the time, especially Doc Savage stories. However, he was aware of the mailman's delivery. After some months, when I commented about receiving another rejection, he exploded in the emotional way he was prone to.

"I'm going to cancel all the subscriptions to those magazines!" he shouted. Unfortunately we didn't subscribe to the magazines to which I sent my stories. But I was greatly touched by his loyalty; it was as good as having a story accepted by the *Atlantic Monthly*, especially since my father was never one to compliment people when they did something special or to apologize when he was out of line. He was too caught up in himself—as his doctor said, on whatever was eating him.

Meanwhile, back on the running track, I earned my varsity letter that year. Little did I know that would be the end of my short running career: The next year during training I suffered a serious leg injury, and I limped around campus for almost a year before I had a complete recovery. By then, my final year in school, I needed to concentrate on academics and part-time work. There was no time for track.

The lessons I learned from running helped me in trying to write: You have to contend with hard work, discipline, pain, and losing (rejection). But if it's important, you'll keep on keeping on.

26

In looking back, I am startled by my commute from home to campus. I never thought about it then, accepting it as the natural order of things the way an innocent child accepts the stars or a budding flower in spring or a newborn puppy—all miracles of their own kind.

The old neighborhood, like many old neighborhoods, has since slid into poverty and neglect that makes the current contrast between South Central Los Angeles and Westwood too striking to ignore. But back then the journey from working middle class to affluent neighborhood was more subtle and therefore seemed something attainable.

I did not know how lucky I was. Very few young people from our neighborhood went to college. A couple of my Irish Catholic friends went to Loyola University. That was about it. In fact, it was enough of a rarity that I can remember the reaction of one particular young neighbor by the name of Marzulo who was older than I was. I hadn't seen him in some time and happened to walk past his house one day when he was sitting on the front steps.

"Hey!" he said. "Whatcha up to?"

He was no great favorite of mine, but I was polite enough to stop and tell him that I was attending UCLA. He was incredulous. He started to laugh. "Hey. Come on. You're just pulling my leg, aren't you?"

It was beyond his comprehension that anyone from our neighborhood could possibly go to college, except perhaps for a year at the city college in order to refine drafting skills and get a job at Douglas Aircraft or Lockheed or North American Aviation. What could I say? I just waved a hand and went on my way. In general, that was the attitude in my neighborhood. Some of the girls, however, thought that a college man might be a good catch.

One of my most memorable recollections of the neighborhood was of a few years later when I was first old enough to vote in an election. I went to the polling place at the local elementary school, a block away, and stood in line. When my turn came up, the woman who later informed my mother about the petition against Mexicans was helping pass out ballots.

My feeling about the two major political parties at that time was "a pox on both your houses!" Like the Catholic Church, the Democratic and Republican parties fell far short of my ideals. When the woman read my party affiliation, she gave me a fishy look, stood tall as a town crier, and barked out in her loudest voice, "Declined to state!" Everyone in the room turned and stared at me. An apostate who wasn't voting the straight Democratic ticket in this Democratic neighborhood? Declined to state? Wasn't that tantamount to being a communist? God! In their urban way they were more closed minded than some of my country relatives in Albuquerque.

To me, the bus ride from South Central L.A. to Westwood represented hope. From little frame and stucco houses with their patch of green to large new California ranch-style homes with hired gardeners. From Sears, Roebuck to Bullock's. From Fords to Buicks and Cadillacs.

The common dream among my friends who attended UCLA was to graduate, get a job that would pay $10,000 a year, and live in Westwood. Beverly Hills and Brentwood we could forgo. But Westwood was attainable, or at least familiar. That's where we went to school.

The realities at that time were a little different. My mother was still working at the defense plant and doling out a weekly allowance that covered my transportation and a few incidentals. I was working part-time. And, as in high school, I had help with my clothing expenses. Not by the ROTC—we never wore uniforms except during class, changing back into civilian clothes immediately afterwards—but the military did have a hand in it.

My Uncle Albert had left his clothes with us when he went into the army and said I could use them on occasion. When he was drafted I was small enough that I don't think he ever expected me to take him up on this offer. But in college I was big enough to wear his clothes, which I did. In those days many young people dressed up instead of down. It somehow gave me the illusion that I was more than scraping by financially. I was a dude. Wool slacks. Sharp sport coat. The result, of course, was that I wore out his clothes so that he had to buy a new wardrobe when he was discharged from the service. When I told him I would replace his worn-out clothes, he smiled indulgently and said it wasn't necessary. He was the uncle who had given me my only childhood bicycle the Christmas I was ten years old, a used two-wheeler that cost five dollars and was my pride and joy.

At the time, my father was acting funny again. His agitation seemed to reach its peak while I was studying for final exams. Those were always tense times for me because so much of the semester grade in a course depended on how well one did on the final. For those courses in which I hadn't applied myself, a poor final exam would have caused my grade to slide from a low B or C to a possible D.

My father seemed to have a wizard's sense of my vulnerability. Or perhaps my own tension about exams resonated on his wavelength. He would be sullen and moody, suddenly lashing out about trivia. He was never much of a drinker, but one bottle of beer seemed to loosen his restraints and tip him into a sort of psychological intoxication.

We could get into an argument about anything. Turn out the lights; don't you know that electricity costs money? Why were you out so late last night—catting around? Then there might be more important issues. You missed Mass last Sunday! Is that what you learn at that godless university? He never seemed to realize that he missed Mass far more often than I did. The arguments that struck deepest at my anxieties had to do with money. I felt dependent. I was not mature enough to see my way to totally supporting myself through school. At such times I hated my reliance on his largess.

At one point he shocked me by telling me that he had been born with congenital syphilis. God knows why he told me. Was I supposed to feel sorry for him? With the self-centeredness of youth, I was concerned only about myself. I asked my mother if I too carried the stigma of that disease. Stiffly, awkwardly, she told me no. I didn't have to worry. I still wondered what other demons lurked inside my father, demons that had a stranglehold on my own being. I would have given anything not to be my father's son.

Over the years I gleaned from the vague shape of unspoken words that my father's father, the grandfather I never knew, had been somewhat of a libertine. I also sensed that he had been something of an autocrat, in that old, cruel Hispanic country way that held a father's word as absolute law—to be enforced by the whip, if necessary.

Then, that demon fading back into the attic like the genie disappearing back into the bottle, the disagreements focused on the more tangible present. When was I going to get a job and earn some money? I was just wasting my time in school. But never a word about the family financial condition. Never a word about how he was feeling the pinch. Never a word about my sister, who was soon to graduate high school and would enter college to stay only a year because of lack of money. Girls didn't have to waste time—and money—getting an education. They just had to get married.

This was one of the times that I responded to my father in a way that frightened me and that I later regretted, when I was mature enough to better understand. "I'm going to finish school!" I said with all the passion of my being. "I'm going to do *better* than you!"

He didn't react. He didn't strike me or curse me. The argument ended right there. I left, trembling, heading out of the house for one of the long walks that I needed to calm my soul while I cursed my father, wondering if when I came back home he would throw me out. Of course, he didn't.

I managed to stumble my way through final exams that semester. Then I headed into the home stretch of completing my premedical requirements.

27

Germany surrendered in May 1945. In August word came that the Japanese had surrendered. I was on the second floor of the chemistry building when I heard the news. I remember opening a window in the laboratory and looking across the lawn toward the physics building with the library next to it, then down to the walks and grass below. The few people outside were cheering and waving their arms. The war was over!

On August 6, 1945, President Harry S. Truman announced, "Sixteen hours ago an American airplane dropped one bomb on Hiroshima. . . . The force from which the sun draws its power has been loosed against those who brought war to the Far East."

Those plain words heralded the unleashing of a power that was to change the world. Three days later another bomb devastated Nagasaki. The Japanese surrendered. Only later did we learn of the havoc, the suffering created by those bombs. But then, that August, there was relief and gratitude that the war was over.

Those of us studying chemistry finally realized the meaning of the rumors we had heard about secret research. In a sense, we were proud to be junior partners in one of the physical sciences that created the world's most powerful force. A more sober assessment was still to come.

When school opened again that fall, a flood of veterans returned from the military to continue their interrupted education or to begin what had been postponed. The GI Bill rewarded them with free tuition and a monthly stipend while attending college: $50 for single veterans and $75 for married veterans.

Almost overnight the population of the campus exploded. Friends who had gone to my high school and were among the returning veterans included

Bill McMillan, Albert Saul, and Jim Taylor. Bill, who had been in the Army Specialized Training Program at Oregon State University (the counterpart to UCLA's V-12 program), had been a lieutenant in the army and remained in the reserve. He was later recalled to active duty during the Korean War and received a bronze star for bravery. Al had not been able to adjust to military life and had received a Section Eight medical discharge. And Jim, my black friend who would later become deputy superintendent of schools for the city of Los Angeles, had been thrust from the less obviously bigoted atmosphere of the West Coast into the segregated army, serving part of his time in the South.

I saw much of Al during this time since he was a chemistry major. His parents had come to the United States from the Isle of Rhodes. They were Sephardim whose ancestors settled in Greece, being among the Jews expelled from Spain about the time Columbus made his initial voyage to the New World. Al's mother, Grandma Saul, spoke what she called Ladino. It was an old-time Spanish with much of the vocabulary identical to that used by my older Spanish-speaking relatives in New Mexico.

Later Al worked as a high-temperature ceramics specialist for a company that designed and manufactured nuclear reactors for producing electrical power. Through some accident or breach of safety, he developed leukemia because of overexposure to nuclear radiation and died at the age of forty, leaving behind a wife and two young daughters. In a sense, a victim of war—or, more precisely, of technology.

It was during this time that my future career began to take shape, despite my obliviousness to it. The return of veterans from the military tremendously increased the competition for grades. These were serious men, many of them older, more mature, and impatient to finish school and get on with their lives. I was finishing up the final requirements before applying to medical school and felt the heat of competition.

Somehow, deep down, I must have had doubts that medicine was for me. I only applied to one school, the University of Southern California, and was granted an interview. The interview was, looking back, a subtle disaster. Here was this callow youth, approaching his nineteenth birthday, being asked why he wanted to become a doctor. To tell the honest-to-God truth, I'd probably never really thought about it before. I mumbled some nonsense about while other kids dreamed of becoming firemen when growing up, I dreamed of becoming a doctor. I could tell from the interviewer's reaction that he didn't believe me. I didn't believe myself.

The next question put a stake through the heart of the whole business. "How are you going to finance this education?" the interviewer asked.

Oh, well. Sure. Yeah. My parents would help out. And perhaps I could work part-time. Carrying a full load in medical school? Fat chance. Go to the foot of the class, Nash. After a nice chat about the courses I had taken, the conclusion was that I should go back and finish work for my degree. Get a few more A's. Apply again. I was still young.

While it was a big disappointment, it was also a relief. Aside from serious doubts about being doctor material, I was just plain sick of school. I did not feel in tune with what I was doing. Science seemed too restrictive to me, being boxed in by facts and *correct* answers, whatever those were. I felt like a mechanical man.

This vague discomfort, this reluctance to commit myself to being a dedicated scientist had slowly crept up on me the previous year. There were other things on heaven and earth that I wanted to know about, including philosophy. I had started by taking a couple of courses in psychology. Then, in the spring of 1947 during my supposed senior year, I enrolled in the most enjoyable course of all those I had taken in college: nineteenth-century American history.

I didn't know what I was getting into. It might be boring. It was one of those lecture classes held in a vast hall that seated somewhere between two hundred and three hundred students. But one fact that intrigued me was that the professor, a man named Brainard Dyer, was the twin brother of Braven Dyer, the sports editor of the Los Angeles Times. A history teacher whose twin was involved in athletics couldn't be all bad. I must have felt some kind of kinship because I was the freak in the Chemistry Department who had been on the track team the previous year.

I don't remember many of the details. What I do remember was the refreshing exposure to the *why* of history as opposed to the *what*, which always seemed to focus on memorizing dates and names. Why did Americans move west? What were the causes of the Mexican War? The Civil War? What were the great undercurrents that propelled history forward? It was exhilarating to learn the reasons why things happened and to relate them to something I could understand. History was not just giant, mythical figures and momentous events. History was me. My family. You. History was *us*. It was as if my skull had been unhinged, lifted open, and the light of the sun forced in.

I read that history text as if it was a mystery novel. Whodunit? To whom? And why? What happened afterwards? And who paid the price for it?

I surmised that we are all walking, living relics of history. Carrying within us attitudes, scars, pains, and the desire for revenge that can take generations to dispel. We are constantly at war with our better selves because of what happened to us or our progenitors. And the most difficult thing of all is for the losers, those who have suffered the most, to be able to forgive—the ultimate human dilemma in striving for heaven on earth. No wonder it takes generations for things to change. Revenge is so much sweeter than forgiveness.

Though I did not know it at the time, this course in history was to have a profound influence on my becoming a writer. It touched a chord in me that wanted to know *why*.

The high point of that exploration of history was the mid-term exam. This was one of those essay types, not the only-one-answer-possible and to-the-third-decimal-point exams I had become so used in the sciences. I don't remember what the question was—I think there was only one. Whatever it was, I was inspired.

The next week, when the graded exams were piled on the professor's lectern to be picked up, he took one paper from the pile and said he wanted to read it to the class. I sat spellbound, listening to my own words come back to me over the heads of two hundred some students. I could see the looks exchanged and the whispered "oohs" and "ahs". I felt as if I would burst. Something important was happening to me. I didn't know what and wouldn't for some years to come.

There was also, of course, the practical matter of what I was to do about college now that I would not be going to medical school the coming year. I did have to take a degree in something—something practical that would make employment possible. The obvious answer was chemistry.

However, feeling the way that I did about school in general, I didn't push it. I stayed on another year, making ten semesters in all instead of the usual eight. The last year was a more leisurely one, completing the few requirements for a chemistry degree while allowing room to broaden myself with nonscience courses in economics and philosophy.

28

Years after I finished college I was reading an article in the UCLA alumni magazine about the low percentage of minority students enrolled during the time I went there in the 1940s. I don't remember the exact percentage. It seems to me that it was on the order of one percent for Hispanic students. In looking through the yearbook of my graduating class of 1948, I counted twenty Spanish-surname students (excluding a few from Spanish-speaking foreign countries) out of a graduating class of more than 1,700. The low number shocked me. But in looking back, especially at those first two years at UCLA, I honestly can't remember seeing another Hispanic student on campus, though there might have been a few whom I never ran into.

It's a strange feeling to be reduced to a statistic, especially such a piddling small one. I never thought of myself as a statistic. I was just *me*, a person like everybody else. It was always somebody else who made me think of myself as . . . what? A statistic? Not exactly. As being . . . I guess the word is *different*. Whenever I had my ethnicity thrust upon me, it was because of someone else's question or reaction. It was a matter of being looked at as *other*. Yet I believed that all men (and women) were more alike than not, just as I believed in the Holy Ghost and the holy Catholic church.

I was sensitized to this early in life, long before I ever went to college. It was because of my father. We differed about this attitude toward self (as well as other selves), and it was one of our lifelong conflicts. He had a keen awareness of the ancestry of others because he was so keenly aware of his own. He had his own internalized pecking order about which we disagreed vehemently. "Lieberman," he might say when a name somehow entered the conversation. Then he'd define it, in this case with a trace of a sneer: "German Jew." Or Tuzinski. Or LaPorte. Or Ennis. Or Calderón. He had an almost compulsive need to define, though not always with a judgmental tone of voice or comment. In doing so, I thought, he was somehow defining himself.

My mother was never concerned about ethnicity. Her general attitude was: I'm me. I'm as good as anybody else. Like it or lump it.

Among my close friends in college, such issues never came up. There were two incidents, though, that forced me to better define myself. Among the members of the track team were two young Anglo men from San Diego. They were friendly, open, and definitely not prejudiced. San Diego, in the southern part of the state, is about fifteen miles from the border of Baja California. This was the same distance I commuted from home to UCLA. With the everyday traffic in both directions across the border, and the numbers of Mexicans who migrated to California, San Diego has a heavy Mexican and Mexican American population.

I don't know how the conversation ever came up, but it did. Was I Mexican? I had never thought of myself in those terms. What relationship did I have to the border? My family was from New Mexico. They didn't migrate to become Americans. We didn't come to America. As it has been said so often, America came to us. I thought of myself as a *New* Mexican—or Spanish, as my father so often declared. But, in disagreement with my father, I accepted the Native American part of me that he always denied. Any fool could look in the mirror and see the obvious.

But Mexican? I did a double take at the question. Then reacted as my father's son. No. Spanish.

No? Well, we have this friend—And he's a wonderful guy—His parents are from Mexico—and—

I felt a great discomfort, as if they were trying to convince me that it was OK to be Mexican. I wouldn't buy any of it. What did that have to do with me? I thought they were being patronizing.

They, in turn, must have thought what so many others have thought: He's denying himself. He's ashamed of it. While all the time they were just trying to be friendly. A failure in communication.

We remained friendly. We continued our season together on the track team. But the question never again came up from them. However, it did later. From someone else.

The GI Bill had enabled ex-servicemen and -women to go to college who might otherwise not have been able to afford it. I noticed more minority students on campus, including Chicanos.

I became aware of a particular group from East L.A. through a young black, a common acquaintance. It was a mixed group: a very pretty young black woman, an exotic young Eurasian woman, and a very Indian-looking Chicano. There were others in and out of the group, but those were the core that I remember. I heard that they, or some of them, or some of the fringe members of the group, were politically active. They reputedly belonged to the American Youth for Democracy, which some said was a communist organization.

Campus politics of the time revolved around struggle for control of student government by the nonfraternity (nonorganized) faction versus fraternity-sorority row. It was, in a sense, the have-nots versus the haves, since the groups split more or less along socioeconomic lines.

It was also a microcosm of politics to come. The California state assembly held hearings about communism on campus during this time. Among the graduates of my class of 1948 was a campus politician named John Ehrlichman, a political science major who was described thus in the 1948 UCLA yearbook: "Pulling wires behind the scenes has kept Kappa Sig John Ehrlichman out of the limelight, but he was a potent political power nonetheless."

Another campus mover and shaker who was to graduate later was H. R. (Bob) Haldeman. On his fraternity's page, the yearbook stated, "Bob 'Happy Harry' Haldeman, the guy with the horrible haircut (crew cut), was the main cog in UCLA's greatest Homecoming Week." Some twenty-five years later Ehrlichman and Haldeman left their footnote to history as members of Richard Nixon's White House and participants in the Watergate scandal.

Campus politics, however, were no concern of mine. As for the politics of the group from East L.A., my attitude was to each his own. But my philosophy was not widely shared. Paranoia about the atomic bomb would soon escalate and become a burning issue among scientists, even scientists-to-be like myself, and would lead into that Alice-in-Wonderland McCarthy era where it seemed that the whole country, or at least the part of it that spoke up, saw evil-intentioned communists behind every bush.

I would see the group gather across the lawn from Royce Hall. Or talking on the steps of the library. We would look at each other and wonder. My young black acquaintance saw this exchange of glances and one day said to me, "So-and-so (the young Eurasian girl) has the hots for you."

That's nice, I thought. She was a pretty young woman. A bit thin for my tastes. But the whole thing was academic (no pun intended). I had no car. No money. No time. Having been raised a good Catholic, I suffered the Catholic neuroticism about sex: "Not until you get married, and even then only to conceive children." The girls I dated were from the neighborhood where I lived, within streetcar or walking distance. Although occasionally I could manage to borrow the car from my father. So there remained these intense, chaste glances across campus, focused now on the Eurasian girl. A certain curiosity. The oft-considered question of what if . . .?

Then one day, as I climbed the library steps, I met the Indian-looking Chicano. I wrote that scene almost directly from life into my first novel:

> Halfway up he sensed a short, dark figure cutting across from the top steps toward him. It was one of the Chicanos from East Los Angeles, a young man that he had seen before among the politicos talking in undertones about whatever it was they talked about. El Chicano was headed right at him, head down, eyes peering up through unkempt hair.
>
> Joe tried to avoid him, but El Chicano stopped immediately in front of him and looked up furtively. "¿Eres mejicano?" Are you a Mexican?
>
> Joe drew back in surprise. He almost blurted out, "Hell no! I'm an American!" when he saw a nervous brown hand clasping and unclasping around a textbook. "Sí," he said instead.
>
> With a quick smile of relief, El Chicano raced down the remaining steps. Joe turned and watched him in amazement. He wanted to laugh. Not at the absurdity of the situation. Nor at El Chicano—he felt a strange sadness that the question even had to be asked. But at his own response. His own freedom to answer. As if the bogeyman that had hung over his father for his entire life, and over Joe for so many years, had disappeared with that simple word: yes.
>
> Yes, he thought. American. Mexican. Human. Ape descendant son of God. Yes. Yes. Yes.

29

One of the greatest sins the Catholic church has ever committed is perpetuating its unhealthy attitude about sex. As a good practicing Catholic in my youth, I, like many others, fought this vicious battle between natural inclination and religious conditioning. While Pavlov's dogs slobbered at the sound of a bell, I drew back from the surge of hormones raging in my blood.

I also sensed my parents' awareness, as they were quietly watching me with worried looks. In a small house it's hard to hide what's going on. Even silence communicates. When I wanted to telephone a girl, I would either wait until my parents were out of the house—which was rare—or go to a pay phone at the drugstore a block away.

Only later, after both of my parents had died, did I completely understand their concern. I learned from their marriage certificate buried deep among their old records that I was born five months after they wed. A vague suspicion had evolved over the years from their failure to ever announce or celebrate their wedding anniversary—at least in a way involving my sister and me. And there was the memory of my paternal grandfather's social disease.

My parents were watching for signs. Would the sins of the fathers be visited upon me? And of course the only conversation about sex that I remember when growing up was initiated by me when I was fourteen or fifteen. I asked my mother a pretty innocent question because my father would have reacted with anger and recrimination.

"Is it all right to kiss a girl if you really like her?"

It startled her only for a microsecond. It was not a dangerous enough question that she would start spying on me for telltale signs of sin. "Why—yes," she replied in the sage tones of a Solomon. "If you really like a girl there's nothing wrong with a little kiss."

That was the extent of my sex education from my parents. The rest came from physical education class in junior high school with stern warnings about venereal disease. And the Jehovah-like warnings from Father Dee, the least likely candidate to advise anybody about sex—or anything else as far as I was concerned. But mostly I learned from the misinformation of friends and from books secretly perused at the back table of the public library, out of sight of the librarian.

During adolescence I was two years younger than my schoolmates and not ready for a social life. I was, in their eyes, backward. I was a puritan, and one of my defenses was to be ultraparticular about the girls I would admit being attracted to. In addition, there was always the question of money and transportation. But nature has a way of overcoming such obstacles.

My first serious romance sneaked up on me while I was attending UCLA. I was dating a schoolgirl who worked part-time at the local Sears, Roebuck with my sister. Her father was a police sergeant, a huge man, who was always in the living room when I called.

One of my neighborhood buddies congratulated me and told me she was supposed to be a hot neck. (Necking was the then prevalent term for making out. God knows what the term will be next year.) Well, that was news to me. For whatever reason, she was always on her good behavior, which, frankly, pissed me off. Maybe college boys were supposed to be gentlemen who only went out with ladies. The thought of her intimidating policeman father looming in the background no doubt also kept me in check. This was definitely not the romance of the ages or even a minor exercise in lust.

A group of us planned to take dates to the UCLA-USC football game, one of those local rivalries that inflamed undergraduates. I asked the policeman's daughter, certain that she would be thrilled. She said no. I don't remember the reason. By God, I thought angrily, that was it!

Having a sister a year and a half younger did have its advantages—I got to meet her friends, including one of her friend's older sister, Juanita. After high school Juanita had gone directly to work as a legal secretary, contributing, I suspect, to the family coffers.

Juanita's parents, who were divorced, had been born in Mexico. In Guadalajara. She, her sister, and a younger brother lived with their mother, an uncle and aunt with at least one daughter that I can remember, and an elderly grandmother. In the two years that Juanita and I went together, I never did figure out the exact population of that house. It was like one of those secretive houses in mystery movies. Silent. With a dark hall. Closed doors that would occasionally open unexpectedly, revealing some character you had never seen before. The occupants whom you *had* met were polite enough, yet seemed reluctant to reveal much about themselves.

I telephoned Juanita, and she said she would be delighted to attend the game. Little did I know what this would lead to. I was so vexed by the policeman's daughter that it didn't dawn on me what a beautiful girl Juanita was until a short time later. It was nothing out of the ordinary at first—just a date.

30

It never registered to me as significant that Juanita's parents were born in Mexico. It never occurred to me that she was the first Chicana that I had ever dated. I never really thought about the ancestry of the girls that I went out with. Or whether or not they were Catholic, for that matter. If there was any bias, it was that they lived somewhere in our general neighborhood or at least within reach by streetcar or bus. I wasn't attracted to a girl because of her ancestry or religion. Good grief. What did hormones know about such matters?

I do remember that my parents had friends, mostly from Albuquerque, who had daughters. Nice Spanish girls. All it took was a gleam of anticipation in an eager mother's eyes to completely turn me off. But most of that sort of thing was to come later when I was a little older and visiting Albuquerque. From the time I was fifteen until I graduated from college I never saw New Mexico; I was either working or going to school.

On our first date, Juanita sat with me and friends in the UCLA rooters' section as a college rah-rah. At halftime the entire section held up colored cards on cue, forming pictures on a billboard-like background. Like my friends, I wore a blue and gold rooters' cap, strictly José College.

She was thrilled to be at the game, not least because her younger sister wanted very much to go but didn't. I remember how Juanita seemed to live college life vicariously when later we would go to the movies and see one of those collegiate musicals that were so popular at the time. Win the game for old Winsockie! Come on, kids; let's put on a dance and save I Owe U from the greedy mortgage holders!

I had the impression that, whether by choice or not, she had forgone college to go to work and help out her family. She was an intelligent young woman, and her sister, who was just a year younger, did go to UCLA.

It didn't take me long to forget the policeman's daughter. Soon Juanita and I were seeing each other on a regular basis and talking endlessly on the telephone. As time went on I found myself not only wildly attracted to her, but also in love. When with her, I was in a perpetual state of heat. And in those days nice girls didn't. And nice boys didn't try—too much.

But it was not always a smooth romance during the two years we saw each other. Like that mysterious house in which she lived, she too consisted of dark halls and closed doors. A few times, out of the blue, she would not want to see me anymore. Was there another man? Someone named Jack? Who was Jack? Was there an unrequited love—someone she could not forget? But there was never any explanation.

During one of these stormy episodes, she telephoned me from work one Saturday morning to tell me it was all off. For emphasis, she had asked her boss, a lawyer, to talk to me. A surrogate father? Her unrequited love? I couldn't figure out what the hell was going on. In the not-to-be-refused stubbornness of youth, I brushed aside their arguments. If there had been some *reason*, like "I don't love you" or "You make me sick," I might have backed off. But it was just . . . whim, I thought, or confusion about the true state of affairs.

One time during this period we went to the theater with her boss, the boss's wife, and another lawyer and wife from the firm. I felt awkward and unsure with these adults, these men of the world. I came off as an immature know-it-all, trying to cover my uncertainty with bravado. I'm sure I didn't pass the office test. "He's not right for you, Juanita," I imagined them to say. "A smartass."

The puzzling thing is that we never argued. There were no big emotional scenes, no angry confrontations. What I began to surmise were our fundamental differences. I sensed that she clung to memories of things she had lost or couldn't have and brooded over them, whereas I wanted to move out into the world, to things that were new, and to forget the past. Material things seemed important to her—like the size and shape of the engagement ring she would eventually have or the desire for a silver tea service. While I didn't want to live poor—remember, I wanted to do better than my father—I didn't need a lot of things. Her family seemed close, stiflingly close from my viewpoint. I was my mother's son: independent of family and intolerant of interference. She was, I'm sure, more mature than I.

But passion is a tar baby. Once touched it's almost impossible to shake. In one of our more placid periods shortly after I graduated from college, I proposed marriage. In those days it was the natural course of events. Young men and women became engaged in their senior year of college, graduated, married that summer, and lived happily ever after.

31

I remember bursting into the house and announcing to my parents, "Juanita and I are engaged to be married!" They had met Juanita, of course. I had brought her over a few times.

They looked at each other in absolute silence. No words of congratulation were offered. Perhaps they envisioned a shotgun in my prospective father-in-law's hands. Or maybe they saw this twenty-year-old kid who looked fifteen and realized how immature I was.

That announcement seeded the storm clouds. It took a while for the storm to break. I don't remember how or when, but it was probably one evening after my father had consumed a beer, allowing him to unleash his darker side.

"I forbid you—" Oh, boy! That's the way to get a willful son's attention. "I forbid you to marry that . . . that . . . Mexican!"

I was shocked. My father the bigot! Jesus—I thought only nightriders on horseback dressed in white sheets were bigots. Of course, I had heard his comments over the years. I remembered how he forbade me to bring my black friend to the house and all that pigeonholing he had done of people based on their surnames. I remembered all that crap about conquistadores.

I was irrational with anger, afraid of what I might do. Rather than argue—what good did it do to argue?—I stomped out of the house for one of those long walks that were so common after a disagreement with my father.

If anything, my father's reaction strengthened my resolve. I couldn't tell Juanita. How could I? The way I couldn't tell my black friend years before. When I would bring her over from time to time, my father's dislike was so obvious that it bordered on rudeness, but he never said anything overt that I remember. I have a faint recollection of my father asking Juanita if she was Mexican with a tone of voice that was heavy with disapproval.

She responded with a frightened look and an inhale of breath as if she had been stabbed. But I'm not certain if this really happened or was my own fantasy because I knew my father's attitude. My mother had accepted Juanita with open arms.

"Your father doesn't like me," Juanita said in anguish. "I want him to like me."

"You're not marrying my father," I replied. "You're marrying me."

The engagement was on shaky ground. This was not the kind of opposition that she bore well. Perhaps it had something to do with her own father, who was divorced from her mother.

Meanwhile, my twenty-first birthday was approaching. Juanita and my mother planned a party for this milestone, inviting all of my friends. It was a wingding of a party. Our house was crowded with young folks dancing to records of the big bands of the time. There was food and drink and laughter. What a wonderful thing, to be twenty-one! My mother, who was forty, had a wonderful time too—as if she was a youngster again. My father behaved himself. At least, I don't recall a scene. It's even likely that he had been out of town, working on the train.

The party lasted into the early morning. Juanita had drunk a bit too much champagne, and her head was reeling. It seemed a good idea for her to stay over rather than have me take her home in that condition.

My mother and I walked her gingerly into one of the bedrooms and put her to bed. Holding her head, Juanita called out my name in a childlike voice. My mother took her hand and turned toward me as if to protect her.

"Leave her alone," she said. "Men are just brutes."

The reaction surprised me. I had no intention of taking advantage of the poor girl or harming her in any way. Perhaps my mother had been talking as if to my father—and about her young self.

The engagement went slowly downhill after that. These two twenty-one year olds—she was six months older than I—were hardly ready for the realities of marriage. At least I know I wasn't. I was working as a chemist and felt that when we married she should quit work. That old-fashioned macho idea that the man should support the family. We argued about that. She was not ready to give up work.

My father's dislike of her angered me. She was a lovely young lady, and he had no reason except blind prejudice to feel that way. What my father thought in no way influenced my own feelings and resolve. But it mattered to Juanita greatly, almost to a point that my father's liking her was a condition for our marriage.

There were other ghosts haunting the scene, old ghosts of hers that I had confronted before, such as not wanting to see me at times—with no explanation. Perhaps there were things she could not tell me, just as I could not tell her why my father disliked her. It was an on-again, off-again emotional roller coaster. I didn't understand what was going on. What had changed? Except for my father's prejudice, I didn't hide my thoughts and feelings from her. Yet she seemed haunted by dark secrets, something—or things—that bothered her and that she could not express, at least to me. Something that she could not let go of.

It couldn't continue that way. I began to have doubts about the match. Would this be the way we lived the rest of our lives? I had seen enough of my parents' conflicts to be wary. Finally, one night when I took her home, we sat in the car and talked. I told her that it couldn't go on like this, that I thought it best for us to break our engagement. I don't remember her reaction, if she had one. Perhaps she was relieved.

We didn't see each other again until just before I entered the Air Force in 1952. I hadn't kept in touch with her nor she with me during the intervening years. I occasionally heard about her from my sister, who was still friends with Juanita's sister. I was dating other young women, but none seriously enough to consider marriage. One evening I received a telephone call from Juanita. She had heard that I was going into the military. They were having a party at her house and wondered if I would come.

Admittedly, I was curious as to why she had asked me. I was also apprehensive, reluctant to open closed doors, to stir cold ashes looking for a spark that might remain. Her family had moved to a large old house in the northern part of the city, but it had that same haunted aura.

I didn't stay long. Juanita met me at the door and introduced me around to friends and family. After a while she drew me aside to talk, leading me to another room, an empty room. She was alarmed that I might be going into danger—it was during the Korean War. I don't remember how it happened, but I could feel her kisses on my face and on my lips. Perhaps I had initiated it.

We stopped abruptly and joined the rest of the party. From across the room her mother walked toward us and confronted me. "What are you doing here, young man?"

Juanita hastily explained that she had invited me. Mother kept a wary eye on me and a protective eye on her daughter. I made small talk for a while, deflecting the family glances, then excused myself.

Juanita walked me to the door, where we exchanged goodbyes. "I don't think this was a good idea," I said. And that was it. Forever.

32

Early in my romance with Juanita, I began my senior year in college. I was still a schoolboy with schoolboy things to do. One of the disappointments of that year was when my honor student friend, Arnold Miller, confronted me. Earlier, he had nominated me for the undergraduate chemical honor society, Alpha Chi Sigma. (Its initials were ACS, the same as those for the American Chemical Society, the professional society for working chemists.) He was very disappointed in me, he said, because my grades weren't good enough; I had been goofing off. Sheepishly, I had to acknowledge that his disappointment was justified. I had no excuse to offer for not doing better except sheer laziness.

His words should have served me as a warning. The most challenging part of the curriculum was ahead: physical chemistry with Dr. Ramsey. This was a must-have course that had to be passed to earn a degree in chemistry. Rumor had it that the grade curve was such that fifty percent of those who took the course wouldn't pass. I thought it an abominable way to treat students who had progressed through three years of the major only to be washed out their final year.

As a result, I didn't take kindly to the lecture course starting that first semester of my last year. I had a strong philosophical difference with the way the course was taught. There were few expository lectures that helped orient and instruct us. In a sense, we were thrown in the water and told to swim. We had to teach ourselves a very difficult subject, guided by a teacher who used the Socratic method to enlighten us. Frankly, it was a bitch!

I felt that it was the most poorly taught class in the entire chemistry curriculum and an extreme symptom of what was wrong with part of the chemistry department. That the best teachers, particularly ones like our organic chemistry professor, Dr. Robertson, did not enjoy the reputation of abysmal teachers who were renowned more for their research than for their concern about students. It was as if teaching and research were irreconcilable, and teaching got short shrift.

The course also required a laboratory session, and, luckily, I was reasonably adept at such work. Unfortunately, the lab instructor, a future chemistry department chairman, and I did not hit it off. I found him to be impatient and overbearing, and he must have thought I was a smart-ass kid.

It made for a very interesting semester. I did, however, earn a solid B in the lab, but did not do well in the lecture course. The final exam in the lecture course tipped my grade to just below a C. A D would require that I repeat the course in order to get my degree. But here dear old Professor Crowell interceded for one of his boys. He talked to Dr. Ramsey, who finally agreed to lower my lab grade from B to C and give me a C grade in the lecture course instead of a D.

The last semester I managed to do well enough in both courses on my own. I also undertook a special undergraduate research project in analytical microchemistry for Dr. Crowell for course credit. For some strange reason, I was considering the possibility of going to graduate school. The message had not yet gotten through to me that I really wasn't cut out to be a chemist. As for being a writer, I never gave it a thought.

On June 17, 1948, dressed in cap and gown, I joined the other graduates who received their diplomas. My mother was especially proud, her eyes shining. Despite all my youthful, ignorant ways, she had stood behind me, encouraging me. Going to work to help pay my way through school. Doing the backroom negotiating with my father, who might just as well have had me quit college and go to work. For a woman born poor in northern New Mexico and who had never completed high school, it was a moment to cherish.

All that remained now was to finally heed my father's words: "Get a job!"

33

The year 1948 was not a good one for college graduates looking for work. Of the fifteen or twenty who received bachelor of science degrees in chemistry from UCLA, only six of us found jobs in the field. A few went on to graduate school to pursue their PhDs. Another one or two went back to school to earn secondary teaching credentials. The rest probably left chemistry.

I was one of the lucky ones. By July I had been hired as a junior chemist in the quality control laboratory of a pharmaceutical company in Glendale, California. The company manufactured parenteral solutions for intravenous feeding of hospital patients. It had been started by a medical doctor some years before and was growing. I suppose my premedical training, including a course in biochemistry, plus Dr. Crowell's recommendation, convinced them. I had just turned twenty years old and looked fifteen.

It was an interesting company—a small family business whose president was, I believe, related to the deceased founder. The assistant sales manager was the president's stepson. The executive vice-president was his son-in-law. I have a vague recollection that the vice-president of sales may have been the president's brother-in-law. Some four years later the family business was acquired by a large corporation listed on the New York Stock Exchange.

The laboratories were not managed by a family member. The director of research and development, who was also a vice president, was a graduate of UCLA. Another UCLA graduate, a biologist a few years older than I, was hired at the same time. This was a liberal company, the biologist told me. He was Jewish—as was the director of R & D—and of course there was me. The biologist had been trying to get into medical school for some time but claimed that there were quotas restricting the number of Jewish applicants admitted to certain schools.

Six months later I was promoted to the research and development laboratory as assistant to the senior research chemist, Dr. W. O. Pool. Bill Pool was to become, unbeknownst to him, a mentor who had great influence on my life.

At the time, Bill was about forty-five years old, thin, and had graying dark hair. He had been born in Meridian, Mississippi, which was rather a shock to the ignorant young man that I was. Somehow, PhDs in chemistry were not born in Mississippi. That was strictly cotton farming and redneck country. He had graduated from "Ole Miss," then received his doctorate at the University of Chicago. He once showed us a photograph from that period. He had grown a full beard like many young intellectuals in the late 1920s and early 1930s. It gave him the look of D. H. Lawrence or the early William Faulkner.

Bill was an inveterate chain smoker, an addiction that would later cost him one lung and eventually his life. His hands trembled incessantly. The only times I can remember calm and steady hands were during company social affairs when he drank liquor. He had an enormous capacity for that. His daytime tremors may have been a result of nighttime boozing.

Bill lived with a roommate, another man, in a large Spanish-style home in Glendale that they jointly owned. Speculation among the young scientists at work—there were two biologists and two of us chemists now—was that Bill was a homosexual. No one knew for sure. It was not a time when people came out of the closet or were militantly gay. Much of our speculation had to do with curiosity about what strange, perverse practices they might engage in. We didn't get it. We were young and ignorant about that world.

Needless to say, Bill was a sensitive and very intelligent person. As a research scientist he was exceptional, able to accomplish a great deal with very little in the way of equipment or fancy gear. The kind of person who, with chewing gum and bailing wire, could work wonders. And his reach of knowledge and interests went far beyond chemistry.

Bill was about the same age as my father, a father with whom I had almost no common intellectual interests. It was difficult having discussions with my father about anything meaningful or controversial. His mind was closed. He may have felt threatened by this son who did not accept his every word as gospel. There was the old New Mexico country, the old Hispanic father-knows-best, shut-up-and-do-as-you're-told attitude that infuriated me. He had enough trouble coping with the world of work without coming home to deal with an argumentative son.

In a way Bill was my intellectual father. I had always shied away from becoming friends with teachers in school. Among family and friends, my father was one of the most educated (having finished high school and a year of teacher's college). Although he was an intelligent man, he was not an intellectual.

At work I had an opportunity to explore ideas and express my thoughts, doubts, and wonders, and not just about chemistry. I would talk about books I'd read and get thoughtful replies—and challenges—from someone who had already read those books and many others.

I can remember talking excitedly about reading Aldous Huxley's *Brave New World*, which was a great discovery for a young scientist. Not only had Bill read it, but he also had met Huxley and had attended some mystical meeting or séance at Huxley's home in the Hollywood hills.

When I discovered William Faulkner's works, Bill had been there before me. When I talked about how difficult Faulkner's writings were to understand at times, he related the anecdote of what Faulkner told someone who had come to him with the same complaint. Read it again!

He was the anvil against which the hammer of my young mind struck, seeking knowledge. I'm certain I wasn't the easiest of assistants. I would argue and disagree. One of my fellow young scientists accused me of being smug. And, as always, I was somewhat reserved, watching silently what was going on around me—a typical writer.

At one company party when Bill had more than enough to drink, he made several pronouncements to individuals present. To the stepson of the company president he said, "You don't know why you're living. All you do is earn a big salary." To me he said, "Still waters run deep." Luckily, Bill was a talented scientist and enough of a company character that people would take it from him and laugh it off. That was just old Bill.

Bill and I had desks in the small research lab with a blackboard on the wall behind my desk, the laboratory benches against the opposite wall. The blackboard would be our playground, where chalk in hand, we'd explore this, that, or the other about the current project or sometimes nonproject.

Once he was trying to get a fresh look at a question, and he postulated how the "pure mind" might approach it. Leave it to young Nash! The pure mind would have no experience on which to make any judgments, I said. It would be blank, like this blackboard, until it learned something. At which point it would no longer be pure. Therefore, contemplating the pure mind was a waste of time. He was quite upset at my closed mind.

Another time, after a similar episode, he started to chuckle and shake his head. "You're the most obtuse chemist I've ever met," he said. He meant I was straight to the point, direct, blunt, as if I had blinders on and could only see straight ahead toward whatever our goal was. Bill, on the other hand, liked to graze around the edges of a problem in case something interesting, out of the ordinary, and significant turned up. He had a playful and creative mind. I just wanted to get the job done.

Another time he looked at me with a mixture of puzzlement and wonder. "You're always so sure of yourself," he said. And, of course, he was not. "Yes," I answered, trying to indicate that sureness of self was not necessarily a virtue, "even when I'm wrong."

When the time came near for me to leave the company, he argued with the director of R & D on my behalf to change my classification to full research chemist. That way, when or if I came back, I would have a better position and a better salary.

"The R & D director is disappointed in you," he said, explaining the convincing he had to do. He meant my work, possibly my lack of ambition as a scientist, and no doubt my immaturity.

"I'm young," I answered, "and still have a lot to learn."

But the most significant thing I remember him saying to me was, "Nash, you have to make up your mind whether you want to be a chemist or a poet." He was right.

34

Work was not mainly about the intellectual education of ignorant young Nash. It was about applying chemistry to the business we were in. It was a business I enjoyed. The people I worked with were intelligent. There was a high level of integrity about the way we went about our work. The products we manufactured were helping save lives.

Not all of my friends felt the way I did. I can remember arguing with some who had only wanted a job that would pay the most money. But I, like many other young people then and now, was an idealist.

One of the very first tasks I was given was to do a library search as background for a research project we were undertaking. Since the resources of the company library were limited mainly to medical reports used by the MD on the staff, I was sent to the chemical library at the California Institute of Technology in nearby Pasadena.

I spent five or six weeks in the stacks, checking and double-checking obscure references and plowing through mountains of journals. One of the prime sources for organic chemistry was *Beilstein*, published, alas, in German. Professor Melnitz, where were you when I needed you? I looked at everything I could find that was even remotely related to our project. I learned a great deal about finding information in a library—something that would stand me in good stead when writing historical fiction. Today it's a lot easier since so much of this data is on computer and in English.

We worked with the people at Cal Tech on other projects. One that I was involved in was the development of a blood plasma substitute called oxypolygelatin, which resulted from chemical cross-linking of gelatin molecules. It was based on some molecular structure research done by Linus Pauling and his team at Cal Tech. Our liaison on the project was one of

Pauling's subordinates. However, I did attend a meeting where Pauling was present. He had a head and bright eyes that reminded me of an alert rooster (not unlike photographs I've seen of the philosopher Bertrand Russell). His intelligence and force of personality were overwhelming. To be in his presence was to know that this was an extraordinary man, especially to a wet-behind-the-ears young chemist. Unfortunately, oxypolygelatin did not turn out to be all that we hoped.

One of our most intensive projects was work on the development of a high-calorie intravenous solution based on dextran, a large molecule carbohydrate that has since been used as a blood plasma substitute. After laboratory and animal tests had established the safety of the product, we did clinical evaluation on terminal cancer patients—who I presume had volunteered—at a Veterans' Administration hospital.

My job was to receive urine specimens from the patients, evaporate measured samples in platinum crucibles, then analyze the residue to gain insight into how the material was being metabolized. What I remember mostly about the project was the stench, going home with the smell of urine on my clothes and in my hair. In chemists' jargon the letter P stands for physical, so that a P-chemist is a physical chemist. Instead, I had become a "pee-chemist."

35

Life was not just work. There was the on-again, off-again romance with Juanita. There was my ambivalence about church. There was the continual head-on confrontation with my ignorance. It was as if every time I learned something new, another door cracked open to give a glimpse of vistas I never imagined existed.

I was not satisfied with my so-called education. I felt that chemistry took a limited view of life, rigid and somewhat mechanical. I did not feel comfortable being a technocrat. There were huge gaps in that narrow picture of the world, important gaps. As we used to say in college about the hierarchy of degrees, "You learn more and more about less and less. BS, MS, PhD—Bullshit, More Shit, Piled higher and Deeper."

The lightning rod for all of these feelings, mostly vague, was my break-up with Juanita. The fact that I had taken the initiative and decided that it wasn't working and never would work in no way assuaged the pain. Suddenly my world crashed in on me. I had never felt so vulnerable to my feelings. And in such a state the world of science seemed even more distasteful. What did it have to do with real life?

There was no one I could turn to for advice. Parents? The parish priest? Friends? Forget it! I was my mother's son, fiercely independent. As I groped to sort my way through the morass, I turned to books to read what others had thought about love, religion, feelings.

I turned to night school to fill some of the gaps in my education. During the four years I worked as a chemist I took eight courses at night of which only one was related to my work.

I took courses in psychology, philosophy, and anthropology. Then, for whatever reason, I took my first writing course: short story writing. Perhaps

I had been writing things down, trying to sort through what was happening to me. Trying to understand. Or perhaps I thought that writing might be some kind of therapy to work through to answers that I didn't find in psychology and philosophy. I don't know.

The writing instructor, like many instructors in community colleges, was not a professional teacher but a person working in the field. Her name was Edna Vann, a middle-aged, somewhat stout woman who had been a story editor in a movie studio and had been secretary to Alfred Hitchcock. She had Hollywood connections, like the instructor of the playwrighting course I later took at USC, whose brother was Cecil B. DeMille.

Miss Edna Vann was something special. She could dissect a story and lay it out in all its disassembled parts for you to see. She talked about beginnings, middles, and endings and capsulizing what a story was about in a few words. I'm sure it was her practical knowledge acquired as a story editor that made her a surgeon of the fictional.

Once she had told us what a story was, reading examples from the best, she asked us to write our own. That first semester's goal was to write one story well. Miss Vann would take home those amateur scribblings, read them, dissect them, and then make suggestions. The final test was for us to read aloud our reworked stories to the class, and then listen to their critiques.

Some were afraid to read. There was one whose words were so precious that he didn't deign to let us hear them. But it was wonderful training, if you could take the heat. Not all the comments were necessarily valid or made sense, but you could sort through them to see if you were communicating. Though admittedly, hearing a story out loud is not the same as reading it while comfortably curled on your favorite chair.

I took to this with enthusiasm. I found that I could lose myself in my writing in a way that seldom occurred with chemistry. There was an emotional side to it that science did not offer.

My first story was titled "The Cry of the Parrot," and I remember keeping count of the rewrites, sixteen in all. The idea for the story came from a fellow employee in my car pool, one of the two passengers I would pick up on my way to Glendale from Los Angeles.

The woman, whose Spanish was better than her English, worked in the export department—the company did a large volume of business throughout Latin America. A widow in her thirties, she had been in the United States but a short time, an exile from El Salvador. Her father had been a justice of their Supreme Court, and he and his family had been driven from the country in one of a never-ending series of political coups that occurred even back then.

She told me about her sister-in-law in San Salvador who had a pet parrot that she had trained to shout, "¡Viva la Revolución!" She was terrified that someone would hear this bird and report her to the authorities, who would arrest her and her family.

I thought it was a wonderful idea for a little horror story that might be submitted to one of the pulps like *Alfred Hitchcock Mystery Magazine*. It would explore the travail of a woman who had trained her parrot to say just those words. The military, ever on the search for revolutionaries, paid her a visit. Luckily, the bird was quiet, but the potential threat was still there and it terrified her. Finally, her fear surpassed her love for her pet, and she strangled it.

I never sold the story. In fact it was to be years before any of my work was published. But the central idea didn't go away. It metamorphosed into a different story titled "Nouvelle Cuisine," which appeared in a collection of my short stories that was published thirty-eight years later. This time the parrot wasn't strangled. It was roasted and served to the military intelligence officer who came to dinner one night.

36

I once read that on the path to enlightenment you must first kill the father, then kill the guru, and finally kill the Buddha. Only then can you achieve independence and autonomy and see the true light.

In a sense, they all represent the same concept: blind authority. I had been struggling and making progress with independence from my parents. My mother helped me by pushing me toward it. I had an unsettled lack of understanding with my father that would continue for years. But I had reached some accord with the fatherland, that is my heritage, which I felt I, unlike my father, had started to come to terms with.

As for teachers, some internal compass had pointed back at me early in life. I somehow understood that no matter what helpers there would be along the way, I would still have to be my own teacher.

Now, of course, it wasn't enough that I had broken up with a sweetheart that I thought I wanted to marry. Or that I had taken the wrong path for my life's work. I had to deal with God.

At the time I did not understand what was happening to me. I stumbled along, half blind, driven by feelings that told me something was not right. But what was it? Was it life—something I had to accept? Was it *them*—whoever that was? Was it me?

I had, like my parents and their parents and so on through the generations, been baptized a Roman Catholic. I had been sent to parochial school in the very early grades until, I suspect, tuition became a problem. My mother was a faithful Catholic all of her life. My father was an on-and-off-again practitioner. More than just a deathbed Catholic, but subject to lapses in attendance at Mass or communion.

When we attended public school, my sister and I were sent to the children's Mass at nine o'clock each Sunday. Afterwards, we would faithfully go to Sunday school for our weekly dose of catechism. We received holy pictures, scapulars, and tiny silver-colored medals for lessons well learned. But memorizing words correctly was not the same as unquestioning faith.

In the early years, when my father was away at work, mother would take us with her to evening services. I especially remember the Friday evening Stations of the Cross during Lent. Father Dee would roll along the aisles in his seaman's lumber, stopping at each of the fourteen painted depictions of Christ's passion along the wall, describing: "Jesus is condemned to death." Or "Jesus meets the women of Jerusalem," followed by the admonition, "Daughters of Jerusalem, weep not for me, but for yourselves and for your children." Whereupon I might look to see if mother was weeping for me and my sister.

Then the other stations with prayers rumbling out in Father Dee's loud voice, occasionally set free by wine that you could smell if you were close enough:

"We adore Thee, O Christ, and we bless Thee, who by Thy sacred cross and passion has redeemed the world."

Followed by more words, then the congregation praying, "Have mercy upon us O Lord Christ! Have mercy upon us!" Followed by the Our Father, Hail Mary, and Gloria.

Then home from church on foot, through the lighted streets of the city, looking into darkened shadows for . . . for what? God the shepherd watching out for his lambs?

I can remember the priest railing against the Jews for killing Jesus. Some of my friends were Jews, and they didn't kill anybody. How could one hate the Jews when Jesus himself was a Jew? What's more, the Romans killed him, not the Jews. What did our Italian friends in the Vatican have to say about that?

And of course, I was told that only Catholics could go to heaven. What about Moisha Candleberg? If I was struck by lightning when playing football with my Jewish friends did that mean I was damned for eternity?

None of this seemed to accord with the doctrine that there was only one God, the God of love. If that was true, we all prayed to the same God. How could he favor only Catholics?

"By their fruits ye shall know them," I was told. I would look at the priest and tell myself: If this is a fruit from the tree of God, something is wrong. I was not yet very tolerant of human weakness, especially in a priest. And forgiveness had to wait a while until I could finally come to complete terms with my father.

It's not unnatural to be drawn to religion when something major has gone wrong in your life. When I broke up with Juanita I began to read about religion, to question more deeply, and to ponder. It reached such a point that my sister had once turned to me in disgust and spat, "Little Jesus!" Meaning what, I don't know. Perhaps that I was going overboard, being more than a little dippy about things.

Like the star that burns brightest just before extinguishing, I became active in the young people's group of our church, even becoming president for a while. The reason was more social than religious, I'm sure. Such groups were encouraged since it brought together young Catholic men and women so they might marry among their own—not unlike my parents' introducing me to their New Mexico friends' Spanish daughters.

We had a good time. Couples used to slow dance then. It was the only way you could hold a newly introduced girl close to you without being accused of being a masher. And the up-tempo jazz music gave you a good workout doing a fast jitterbug.

We attended dances at other parishes, widening our circle of potential mates. It was at one such dance that I met Maureen. She was attending Catholic Marymount College, studying to become a schoolteacher. She was to become another dilemma in my young life, as I was no doubt in hers.

37

Maureen was a pretty girl whom I enjoyed dating. To her I was this boy who had finished college young and liked to do different and interesting things. Not just the dances, parties, and picnics of the church group, but more cultural interests. Things that were new to her—and me. The theater, foreign movies, jazz concerts.

She was a good Catholic and had received a parochial school education. Not least, I believe, because her father was *not* Catholic, for she expressed to me more than once that she wished he would join the church. Like my father, her father was a supervisor in the Postal Service, working at the Post Office rather than on the trains. Her mother was a schoolteacher.

Since she was four years younger than I was, our relationship blossomed slowly. We never went steady, but we saw each other fairly often. After Juanita, I was not ready for a serious relationship.

Though still a Catholic at the time, I had my doubts, which grew stronger as time passed. It had nothing to do with trying to live a moral life. (As a boy, I had fleetingly considered the priesthood—much as I had considered West Point in high school.) There were just too many things about the dogma that I found hard to accept.

There were a few other college graduates in the parish. Some of the young men I knew had attended Loyola University. Through them I was invited to attend a meeting of male Catholic college graduates. It was a bizarre experience. The Jesuit philosophy teacher led us in a discussion that turned into a question and answer session, ostensibly to prop up the faith of these overeducated altar boys and keep them in line.

As had been my wont, I was among the first to ask a question—a question that was no doubt on everybody's mind, but one that few were foolish enough to ask. It was a tendency that had gotten me into trouble more than once in school. I don't remember the question now, but it was a heavy one—a sword thrust at the heart of belief. Probably something to do with the relation of science to religion—perhaps reconciling the Adam and Eve story with scientific theories about the evolution of the planet. The others in the group burst into laughter at the audacity of such a thing.

The Jesuit leaped at a chance to respond. "This is just my meat!" he proclaimed, drawing himself up to full height. Then he went on to an explanation in a loud and emphatic voice that silenced the laughers but left me incredulous. It was like listening to a martian, to a man from outer space. I couldn't believe the convoluted rationalization. It was like listening to someone explain the reason for the different colors on the wings of the angels standing on the head of a pin. Once you are bullied into accepting a false premise, anything is possible. I had been reading much during my formative years, starting with the usual high school English assignment crap, much of which I found boring. The first really good writing that had turned me on was James Joyce. I found in some of his work a lot of what I thought and felt in first questioning, then rejecting Catholicism. I never went back to that group. My suspicions were confirmed.

All this was happening while dating Maureen. Catholicism's hold on me was loosening. As time went on I became wary of anything serious with her. She was a devout Catholic, and I could not see being subjected to the same wishes she held for her father. I could never see raising any children of mine as Catholics. It was one of those friendships where we were both attracted to each other, but it was going nowhere. It never got to the point where we even discussed the problem of religion.

I don't remember exactly when I made my final break with the church. It must have been sometime between my twenty-first and twenty-second birthdays. What I remember is that it ended not with a whimper but with an act of defiance, one that was not unlike the experience of the character Irene Bustamante in my novel *A Daughter's a Daugher*:

> Then the tinkle of the bells called those who had confessed and been absolved, those who had fasted, to receive communion. It had been a different call for Irene. A call of emancipation. She had not made her confession. She would accept the host, the transubstantiated body and blood of Christ,

while in this state, risking hell and the wrath of heaven. It was, for her, a matter of life or death. If she was to commit this sacrilege and her disbelief in things Catholic was mistaken, then the heavens would part and a bolt of lightning would strike her dead. How could it be otherwise for someone who defied God?

When the bell tinkled again and the last stragglers made their sleepy ways toward the altar, Irene felt one last pang of fear. It was now or never, she thought. God will either strike me down or he/she is just another superstition.

It was the longest journey she had yet taken in her young life. The earth had stood still, stretching out those seconds of agony and doubt and fear and defiance. Until she was at the altar railing, forcing herself to kneel. Clutching at the railing to fight her sense of vertigo. Forcing her head backward as if it weighed a ton. Forcing open the dry, trembling lips. Hearing the mumble of Latin above her. Seeing the thick, sausage fingers loom before her eyes, the white host between them. Feeling the wafer on dry tongue. The sudden gulp, then a second attempt to swallow before she rose and walked on trembling legs back up the aisle.

Now! she thought. Now the lightning will strike. All the way up the aisle that thought shouted to her. Until she had reached the pew from which she had started, still unsinged, still alive. But there was no sigh of relief. There was instead a slight tinge of disappointment and a sense of loss that she did not want to acknowledge. Life would never be simple again.

38

The military was never very far away in those days. While World War II had ended in 1945, there was still military conscription. I had a student deferral while finishing college and, on graduation in 1948, I enlisted in the U.S. Naval Reserve. The alternative was to be drafted and to postpone my career as a chemist. As a matter of fact, a program like the naval reserve to keep me out of the service was a condition of my employment.

I attended regular reserve meetings in Hawthorne, California. One summer I went on a training cruise to Pearl Harbor aboard a destroyer. But again, the military was less and less my thing. Especially since the country was at peace, tenuous though it might have been at the time.

After fifteen months my attendance at reserve meetings dwindled down to nothing. There were other things I preferred to do. Not attending meetings would eventually make me subject to the draft. However, my work as a research chemist qualified me for a deferment based on having an essential job.

I don't remember exactly when I applied for a deferment from the draft. I do remember that a military officer, a friend of our director of R & D, came to the laboratory to interview me. To find out, as he said, what I did that made me so deferrable. The Korean War erupted in June of 1950, and at that time I had a deferment that kept me out of the military.

In the meantime, of course, the seeds of change in my life had been planted. The one that grew with greatest force, like a weed pushing its way up through a crack in the sidewalk, was the question of career. My boss, Bill Pool, was right: I had to decide whether I wanted to be a chemist or a writer.

In retrospect all decisions look easy. As Bill Pool had said, I had never been one to agonize over making decisions. I was obtuse. But I must have thought about this one long and deeply. My mother had encouraged and worked to help me through college. My father had tolerated my independence, my move away from how he thought I should act and think. Now I would throw that all away—for what? I didn't know for certain. But I was happiest working on my writing, much happier than working in a laboratory, which as far as I was concerned was just a job. Writing seemed to fulfill all of me, something that chemistry did not.

I decided that in order to make this change I would have to resign my job, fulfill my military obligation, then move on to my new field of work. When I announced this to Bill Pool, who in turn announced it to the director of R & D, they had a suggestion: They could reshape my job so that I could do more writing in the laboratory. I never for a moment considered this as an alternative. I needed to make a clean break.

There were, as usual, complications. About that time I had a laboratory accident and seriously burned my lower left arm. It had to do with bottles and carelessness, not unlike the incident in Professor Crowell's laboratory when I was in college. But this time the bottles were filled with a solution of carbohydrate and sealed. The solution of carbohydrate was being hydrolyzed in an autoclave, a high-pressure steam cooker of the type used in hospitals for sterilizing. I was running late that day and reduced the pressure and temperature of the autoclave too rapidly. The glass bottles were under high pressure. As I opened the autoclave door, they exploded, spewing shattered glass and sticky, hot solution around the laboratory.

At the noise everyone came running in, expecting to see blood and pieces of Nash splattered on the walls. Miraculously I suffered not a single cut, but my left arm had been soaked with the solution, like a weakened version of non-flammable napalm.

The burns would heal in time. I took the incident as an omen. If I overstayed my welcome in a chemical laboratory, some damned bottle was going to get me some day. I was not cut out to be a chemist.

I made my rounds of the military services to find out what programs, if any, might make sense for me. The navy wanted a five-year enlistment. Forget it! The air force wanted a shorter lease on my life. And there was, the air force recruiter said, the possibility of being assigned to Wright-Patterson Air Force Base to work at chemistry. My education and experience wouldn't be a total waste.

When my friends at work heard that I resigned to enter the military, the young men told me in polite language that I was crazy. Several of them were opposed to the UN action in Korea, and obviously I wasn't. Two of them had been in the service during World War II and had nothing kind to say about military life.

When I announced my intentions to neighborhood and church friends, one pretty young colleen pleaded with me about my future career. "Oh, please," she said. "Don't write about racial prejudice." It was not a subject that I gave much thought to at the time. In looking back it seemed more a concern of hers than mine, to be reinforced years later by a comment from a fellow worker of Irish ancestry who read my first novel just after it was published: "Mexican Americans are not the only ones in this country who have suffered racial prejudice."

With a waiver on my burned arm from my doctor as well as those of the air force, I passed my physical. On August 19, 1952, healed and ready to go, I was called to active duty in the air force as a second lieutenant.

39

My parents were concerned, but they accepted the fact that it was my decision to make. Juanita had heard and gotten in touch with me after some two years; that was our final goodbye. Maureen and I were friends, nothing else, and we agreed to write; she was finishing college.

I did have a plan—more or less. I intended to complete my military service, apply for the University of Iowa graduate writing program, then attend on the GI Bill if I was admitted.

My first stop was Lackland Air Force Base, San Antonio, Texas, for six weeks of officers' basic training. I joined a contingent of other young second lieutenants. Almost all of them were college ROTC graduates and brand new shavetails. I was one of the few directly commissioned officers and, for once, a couple of years older than most of my classmates.

My stay in Texas was a blur. I can remember playing tennis with my roommate in 105-degree weather, showering, and then going to the officers' club to "rehydrate" with several beers. I can remember driving to Austin with this drunk wild man from the University of Arkansas to cheer for the Razorbacks in a football game with the University of Texas. I can remember driving to Corpus Christi with a friend from Los Angeles, a sergeant stationed at a nearby air base, fearful for my life as he zoomed along the straight, endless Texas highway between 90 and 100 miles per hour. I can remember meeting the daughter of an air force colonel at the officers' club and having dinner at a quaint restaurant along the San Antonio River. I can remember visiting the Alamo with some buddies, and then once again with my worried parents who took a vacation trip to San Antonio to see Texas, they said—but I knew they really came to make sure that I was all right.

Most of all, I remember assignments after completion of basic training. There would be no Wright-Patterson Air Force Base for me. No other appropriate assignments for others in the class. Not for my roommate from Dartmouth, who hoped to get into engineering. Not for my fellow Californian who had studied to be an architect. Not for the brilliant but neurotic mathematician who tried to get over on anyone anytime he could. Nor for my good-ol'-boy pal from Oklahoma who had supplemented his college allowance as the fraternity house bootlegger, slipping over into a wet county in Texas to run booze back to dry Oklahoma.

Everybody—the entire class—was going to ground electronics school. Never mind what a recruiting officer told you. Everyone knew that recruiting officers were total liars. And the above-mentioned young men and I were to be roommates off base when we arrived in Biloxi, Mississippi, for training as radar officers.

The uproar was instantaneous and strident. Then, after a while most of us decided, what the hell! It might be interesting. It was different. Who knows? But one young lieutenant in our squadron insisted that he had been betrayed. The government had promised! He wasn't going to take this lying down! They were ruining his life! He immediately complained to his father, who knew a U.S. senator. Suddenly, one morning, he was gone without leaving a trace. We had one less young second lieutenant to put up with. He was discharged for the good of the service.

The rest of us did not look too kindly on that young man. None of us were wildly enthusiastic about the military, but we figured it was our job. Our turn. We would tough it out, even being assigned "overseas" to Mississippi. There were people we knew, like my friend Bill McMillan, who were really overseas, putting their lives on the line in Korea.

40

I had never been in the South and knew it only from hearsay. Although Texas might be called south, it was also west, and San Antonio was as much Mexican as anything else. Biloxi is on the Gulf Coast and is flat, beautiful country that is warm all year round and hot—and humid—in the summer.

Even though the state's population was largely black, I rarely saw a black person in town. It was strange, as if there was another, hidden town in a different dimension, in a place warp that required a password for you to enter.

The base busily trained airmen from all over the world. There were officers from Marshal Tito's Yugoslavia wearing the bright red communist star above the visors of their hats. Our class of a dozen included two Filipino officers. The more lively of the two, Sixto de León, must have learned some of his English from old Mickey Rooney movies. He peppered his words with out-of-date American slang, showing us that he was "with it," a real "hepcat."

With the base so crowded, some of us had to find living quarters off base. Five of us lucked into a cottage in a small vacation motel next door to a restaurant, the Friendship Inn. You could look across the highway to the fine sand and the flat, placid gulf, unlike the roaring Pacific surf in Southern California. Flat-bottomed boats whizzed by, driven by propellers mounted on the deck like giant fans. At night you could see people with their baited nets and flashlights crab fishing.

It was a time when Senator Estes Kefauver of Tennessee was investigating crime in America, yet you could go to a hotel just down the highway from Keesler Air Force Base and find open gambling. Mississippi was a dry state, like Oklahoma and certain counties in Texas. But the restaurant next door to our cottage openly served liquor, and I often bought a six-pack of beer over

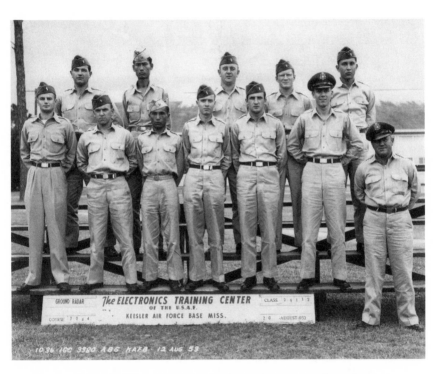

Nash (far right, back row) and his fellow classmates in electronics,
Biloxi, Mississippi, 1953

the bar. On the top of each can, stamped in blue, was a notice from the state of Mississippi that the state tax had been paid.

Electronics classes were held on base from seven in the morning until noon. Afternoons were reserved for study since this was a fairly intensive course. The goal was to prepare us to man radar sites in remote areas and to operate and maintain the equipment. Lectures were held in rooms just under the roof of old airplane hangers. When it was hot and humid, our khaki shirts would be soaked with perspiration by seven thirty. After lecture we'd go down on the ground floor of the hangar and get hands-on training with equipment. One of the most important safety lessons was to keep one hand in your trouser pocket while poking around troubleshooting a radar set. The Air Force wasn't interested in spending money training second lieutenants only to have them electrocute themselves by reaching across high voltage circuits.

Mississippi was another world from country New Mexico and urban Los Angeles. Except for my ex-boss Bill Pool, I had never known any southerners. Most of the migrants I had gone to school with in California were from midwestern states, such as Iowa and Nebraska, or were kids whose families had come from the dust bowl of Oklahoma during the 1930s.

Many of us nonsoutherners had attitudes limited by exposure to books and movies like *Tobacco Road* and *Gone with the Wind*. Many of us thought in stereotypes. I had already had some preconceptions shattered by Bill Pool, and others were put to rest by fellow student officers, such as one who was a Phi Beta Kappa and a Little All-American football player from the University of the South in Sewanee, Tennessee. Not that there weren't problems. One Saturday night a discussion about race escalated to argument and then to a fistfight between some Yankee officers from the North and some local Reb lieutenants. After this one incident, things simmered down, albeit tenuously.

We settled into the routine. Classes in the morning, study in the afternoon, and the occasional recreation—tennis or golf on the green where Woodrow Wilson was said to have played.

For single young men, dating was scarce. The ratio of men to single women was overwhelming. There was a girls' school nearby, a finishing school for young ladies where airmen with the proper credentials were allowed to call. "Proper credentials" meant letters from a former employer and a minister attesting to our moral rectitude. My former director of R & D dutifully replied to what he referred to as "that quaint request." One visit to the school was enough. I was on the wrong wavelength for such social innocence.

I did discover the Biloxi library—and the younger of the two librarians. She, however, was going steady with Captain Somebody-or-Other, but at least we could talk about books.

It was in that library that I discovered a copy of a private edition of William Faulkner's "Notes of a Horsethief," later included in his novel, *A Fable*. As I remember, the copy was numbered as one of about 1,000 that had been printed, and it had been signed by the author.

I was a Faulkner fan since first discovering his work. It moved me powerfully and was almost always worth the effort to grope through his prolix and sometimes difficult-to-follow prose. When it was working, it was like a particle whirling in a cyclotron, the energy forcing the particle round and round, faster and faster to almost unbearable intensity. He was then and remains for me now the finest American novelist of the twentieth century.

I shared my enthusiasm for Faulkner with the older librarian, a woman of about sixty. We had talked about books before, and she knew that I aspired to be a writer. With true loyalty to her state and her heritage, she said, "Well. He's a fine writer and all, but you mustn't believe all those things he says about Mississippi."

41

It may have been the inspiration of being in Faulkner country or perhaps that was merely the added push I needed, but I began to write my first novel. Classes filled my mornings, followed by lunch at the officers' club, but the afternoons were entirely open—supposedly for study. I had no ambition to be the brightest radar officer in the air force, and I already had enough background in physics and math to get by without studying too hard. I saw the afternoons as an opportunity. I had never before had so much potentially free time to write. All I had to do was reach out and take it.

I took my pencil and paper to the library in Biloxi—which was small, quiet, and conducive to writing—or, on days of beautiful weather, I parked myself on a bench outside of our cottage.

This was the first of seven novels I would write before my first published book, *Memories of the Alhambra*. I've thankfully forgotten the title for that manuscript. It was a perfectly horrible novel that I had the good sense to destroy some time later.

About that time I became aware of a published first novel written by young white Mississippian Jefferson Young. Titled *A Good Man*, it had a black protagonist and received excellent reviews. I enjoyed it immensely. It showed another side of Mississippi life, more benign and less intense than the Faulkner works I had read and less mysterious than this blackless South I saw in supposedly black Mississippi. This must have been in late 1952 or early 1953. It would not be until 1954 that the Supreme Court ruled in Brown vs. the Board of Education that schools had to be integrated, and not until 1957 when the Little Rock confrontation required Federal troops to enforce the law. It was during this later time that my literary hero, Faulkner, would be vilified by segregationist Mississippians, including family and friends, for speaking out about the need for change. A book like *A Good Man* seemed to be a straw in the wind.

Sometime during that period I saw Jefferson Young stagger out of the bar next door. I wondered if the book had been all that he wanted it to be—or had perhaps been too much. I don't know if he ever published another novel.

I decided to stay in Biloxi over the Christmas and New Year's holidays. My roommates went home on leave, and I had the cottage to myself to write. It also gave me time to submit an application to the University of Iowa, even though I did not know when I would be able to attend.

There were few officers in our class who remained on base that holiday, so the environment was conducive to writing and contemplation. The writing went well—even on a terrible novel the writing can go well. Somehow I managed to acquire two tickets for the Sugar Bowl football game in New Orleans on New Year's Day. I invited one of the Filipino officers to attend, thinking perhaps he'd like to see a little more of American culture. His compatriot, Sixto, had gone to visit some friends out of the area.

I don't remember the officer's name, but I can still see him. He was a little fellow, barely five feet tall, and he had a dark complexion with features that looked slightly Asian. I could envision him in a loincloth somewhere deep in the jungles of the Philippines, stalking his prey with a blowgun or a spear. He was a quiet little fellow, not like his taller, bubbly pal, Sixto, who was always amusing us.

I had never thought before what he and Sixto might know and think about American racial attitudes, especially here in the Deep South. I found out as we drove the eighty miles to New Orleans. As I steered the car into the stadium parking lot, my passenger became obviously agitated. Finally, as I was parking, he turned to me.

He had heard about how they treat Negroes in the United States, he said, About how they were not allowed to enter certain places. About other terrible things. Well, he said, no one had better mistake him for a Negro and give him any trouble. He undid the lower button of his khaki shirt and pulled out a small automatic pistol. He allowed me a flash of a look, tucked the pistol back into his waistband, and rebuttoned his shirt solemnly.

Jesus, I thought. What have I gotten myself into? Was I about to be a party to an international incident? I could see headlines in the *New Orleans*

Times-Picayune: "Filipino Officer Shoots Local Redneck While Thousands in Sugar Bowl Watch in Horror."

Luckily there was no incident. But that afternoon my adrenalin-charged heart was pumping faster more for thoughts of my pistol-packing companion than for the excitement of the football game.

The new year was much like the old: morning classes, afternoon writing and some study, and occasional crumbs of social life. The Gulf Coast was a resort area, mainly attracting people from the cold, snowy Midwest. On occasion a rare flower from wintry Chicago or points thereabouts would make her appearance at the motel where we lived, much to our pleasure. She would enjoy being the center of attention of young air force officers almost as much as we would enjoy her company.

The months passed and the fighting in Korea continued. The Eisenhower administration had taken over the reins of government that January with the new president's promise that "I shall go to Korea." There were endless and futile talks of negotiation. Then finally on July 27, 1953, the armistice was signed.

We graduated from electronics school on August 20, ready for permanent assignments. Like the rest of the class I had received my orders. I would be going to a radar site somewhere in the wilderness of Puget Sound in the vicinity of Seattle, Washington.

Then lightning struck! All orders were put on hold. All plans were changed. With peace declared, we were given the choice of signing up for four more years of duty or being discharged immediately. That was no choice. In September of 1953, I, like most others of my classmates, was released from active duty although I was to remain in the air force reserve for another nine years.

Second Lieutenant Nash Candelaria, circa 1953

42

There was the long drive back home to California, and I spent most of it bleary eyed while crossing that vast state of Texas. But adjustment to civilian life was not hard. I had never really been anything other than a civilian. The most difficult thing was fitting into my civilian clothes—too much beer and soft living had added a few pounds around the middle.

My parents were relieved. I would no longer face the possible risk of warfare. My sister had married a Los Angeles policeman while I had been away. Maureen and I were still friends, but at a polite distance. Her reply to one letter I had written while I was in Mississippi brought me up short. I was just lonely, she had answered. That's why I had carried on about how much I missed her. She was right, in the truthful and unsentimental way women often are about such things.

By this time I had finished my first, no-name novel, and had put it away to age. Perhaps I was hoping that some miracle would transpire and turn it into something readable. I had my air force pay, accrued leave pay, and the travel allowance to return home, which would keep me solvent for a few months after compensating my parents for room and board. It was a wonderful opportunity to do some more writing before going back to work.

A short trip to Guaymas, Mexico, with a friend inspired the setting for my next effort. I plunged in. It was a novel about fishing and sex, a pseudo-Hemingway mishmash. Another clinker. Mercifully, this one, too, I destroyed—sooner rather than later.

By this time I had heard from the University of Iowa that I had been admitted to their graduate writing program. The thought of returning to academia was not appealing. Nor was the thought of living on the GI Bill stipend of seventy-five dollars a month. I politely withdrew my application.

After a couple of months it was time to get back to earning a living. My friend Albert Saul suggested that I apply where he worked. The Atomic Energy Research Department of North American Aviation, Inc., later to become North American-Rockwell, was designing nuclear reactors for production of electric power. Then noncontroversial, atomic energy was one of the waves of the future. The company's research group needed a writer-editor who understood chemistry and physics and could help scientists with their reports and proposals. My education and experience were ideal.

Because this work was being done through the auspices of the Atomic Energy Commission, I had to wait for my atomic energy security clearance, a "Q" clearance. Since I already had a secret clearance from the air force, I was eligible to work on other projects within the company. Thus I was temporarily assigned to write and edit about aircraft that another division of the company manufactured.

One of the writer-editors in the aircraft group, an Anglo as we would say in New Mexico, was active in party politics in Montebello, one of the predominantly Chicano suburbs east of Los Angeles. It was from him, in early 1954, that I first heard the word Chicano.

Just what is a Chicano? The answer you get will probably depend on whom you ask. The definition includes political, cultural, and class (which in the United States means money) aspects. One of the clearest definitions appears in the delightful book of essays, *Drink Cultura: Chicanismo*, by my late friend José Antonio Burciaga.

Tony describes *Chicano* as follows: "Anyone born of Mexican ancestry in the United States. It includes those whose ancestors go back to the Indio-Hispanic roots of the Southwest. It can also include those born in Mexico or other Latin American countries but raised in the United States who identify with Chicanos."

There are others who have maintained that *Chicano* means those who in addition resist assimilation into U.S. Anglo culture. Some, like a few of my relatives, reject the word *Chicano* for *Spanish*, preferring to ignore the Indian part of their ancestry.

I prefer Tony's definition, especially when appended by his further comments: "A Chicano is both Hispanic and Indian. . . . Our ancestors are not only the conquistadores, but the conquered. It is our vanquished heritage that has always haunted us and been ignored."

But in 1954 the word *Chicano* did not hold significant meaning for me. During this time I wrote fiction on occasional evenings and weekends—I was by no means a fanatic. I wrote my first almost-published short story, "Tío Enrique's Coffin." It was my first story set in New Mexico, and it was based on a family anecdote my mother had told me about her maternal grandfather.

Julian Dalton, Spanish-speaking and New Mexican in all but surname, lived in the area of Pecos in northern New Mexico. Even today Pecos is a small rural village where life goes on much the way it has for decades. Like many people in the small, poor, isolated villages in the mountainous north of the state, Julian was very independent and self-reliant. Since the life he lived was hard, he wanted a better send-off to the hereafter. So, as he got older, he spent much of his spare time carving himself an ornate wooden coffin.

I sent the story off, hopeful of publication. No magazine was interested until I received a note from one whose name I forget. A magazine headquartered somewhere in the Southwest and probably long since defunct. They liked the idea and had a few suggestions. If I wanted to rework the story and resubmit it, they might see their way to publishing it.

I read the letter with mixed feelings: I was elated at the possibility of being published, but I was not so sure about their suggestions. It was as if they were trying to write the story for me, trying to slant it in a way that made me uncomfortable. To make a social comment that had not been my intention.

I showed the letter to Albert Saul, half thinking that, hell, I just might make those revisions. It was tempting. But something about the name of the magazine was vaguely familiar to Al.

There was intense turmoil in nuclear science at the time. The scientific community was gravely concerned and split over the moral aspects of the bomb. Robert Oppenheimer was undergoing his ordeal: After leading the team that developed the atom bomb, his patriotism and right to a government security clearance were under attack, and he finally lost his clearance in June of that year.

It was at the height of this country's anticommunist hysteria. There was fear that the Soviets would develop their own nuclear weapons. The Rosenburgs had been tried and executed for passing atomic secrets to the Russians in June of the previous year. Senator Joe McCarthy was conducting his witch hunt and was finding communists under every bed and in every broom closet.

A day or two later Al came back to me with his report. The magazine was on the U.S. attorney general's list. This meant that they were either communists, communist sympathizers, or subversive—at the very least they were suspect. Not exactly a magazine in which someone with a Q clearance should be publishing, he said.

Now I better understood the changes the magazine's editor had suggested. Changes I did not embrace on artistic grounds. I did not revise the story. It was never published, but a few years later I expanded the story to a short novel and it is the only manuscript from that early period that I did not destroy.

43

I stayed with the Atomic Energy Research Department for about a year. Then I moved on to another job in Fullerton, California, that offered better prospects and a better salary. It was a company in one of the new businesses resulting from the explosion of technology after World War II, the manufacture of analytical instruments for chemical laboratories. The business—and company—was quite small at the time and was growing at the kind of rate that made Wall Street investment managers' mouths water. It was one of the hot young companies in the country.

The company was young in another way too—its personnel. Though founded by a venerable professor who had once taught at Cal Tech and who was chairman of the board, the analytical instrument part of the business was under the general management of a twenty-eight-year-old whiz kid. It was almost as if the professor had put one of his graduate students in charge. Others in the company were comparably young, all driven by ambition and zeal.

It was an exciting place for young scientists and engineers to work. New ideas led to new commercial, high-powered instruments that were helping advance research in laboratories throughout the world. As a young technical writer schooled in analytical chemistry, I wrote instructions for operating and maintaining the new instrumentation. My supervisor, who was to become a close friend, was a thirty-year-old ex-journalist named Lew Hodgson who was to die of cancer by the time he was forty.

While science and career may be exciting, the most important thing about the company was that it was where I met my wife. Doranne Godwin had moved from Henderson, Nevada, a small town south of Las Vegas that had been thrown together during World War II to process magnesium and other ores for the war effort. A temporary town that, like so many others, became permanent. She had joined the company as a secretary for the market research manager three months before I was hired.

I no doubt first saw this beautiful young woman in the cafeteria during a coffee break. I remember Lew Hodgson teasing me, a single young man, about the single young women at work—Doranne in particular. He nicknamed her "Kewpie doll" because of her pert round face and the fact that neither he nor I knew her name. Later, when I got to know her and Lew would see her, he'd tease me by whistling a ballad from the then popular musical *Oklahoma*, entitled "People Will Say We're In Love." In a way, if you can say that couples have their song, that was ours.

But first I needed to meet her. I never had any dealings with the market research department. But thank God for books! I was in the company library one day, searching for some scientific reference or other, when I rounded the corner of one of the bookcases and found something much better. There she was, also searching the literature.

I can't honestly say that it was love at first sight—I *had* seen her before. But I was struck—no doubt about it. I don't remember what I mumbled, or what she said in return, though I'm certain I had the good sense to introduce myself. I didn't wait too long before I telephoned and asked if she would meet me in the cafeteria for coffee the next morning.

I had told her that I was a writer. I'm not certain that she really believed me. Perhaps she thought it was just another line by a young man trying to impress a young woman. When I met her for coffee, I brought along a draft of a short story in progress to show her.

I don't remember what we talked about. I was nervous and quite taken with her. I felt the eyes of others in the cafeteria looking us over. What I do remember was that somewhere in the middle of our conversation she looked straight at me and said, "Don't look at me like that."

"Like what?" I said, startled.

"Like you want to eat me up."

I burst out laughing. The cheeky young thing! I was both embarrassed and amused—and hooked.

In looking back—that was 1955—we never quite agree on the details. Doranne claims that I proposed marriage on our first date. No, I replied, I'm not that rash. It was our second date.

There were, of course, a few things to consider. She was uncomfortable about dating someone from work and especially sensitive to possible gossip. There was also a more basic issue.

Before she rented her own small apartment she had stayed temporarily with the aunt of an uncle of hers, a Catholic who had married her mother's younger sister. Aunt Lettie was the housekeeper for the priests in a parish in the nearby city of Whittier. Doranne had been brought up a Protestant, primarily Presbyterian. While not prejudiced against anyone's religion, she was concerned about the religious education of any children she might eventually have.

Was I Catholic? It was a reasonable enough assumption.

No, I said. Not any more.

Did I intend to raise any children of mine as Catholics?

Definitely not!

She was quite relieved. She was really a heathen like me. One who rejected institutional religion. What you might call a cultural Judeo-Christian who preferred to eliminate the middleman and speak directly to the great power beyond. We were religious soul mates though we came from different ends of the spectrum. We would never have arguments like those described in Joseph Heller's novel *Catch 22*, where Yossarian and his sweetheart were terribly distraught because the God she didn't believe in was not the same as the God he didn't believe in.

Religion was the last thing on my mind at the time. I was just plain smitten. However there was another concern, one that was painful for Doranne to bring up. She had moved to California from Nevada after a short, youthful, very unhappy marriage that lasted about a year and a half. She had refused any kind of financial settlement or alimony just to be free of it.

I don't remember exactly how I reacted. It was something to consider. You always wonder why things don't work out. I know it gave me a few sleepless nights. But as I got to know her better, any doubts I may have had disappeared. People make mistakes. I was certainly aware of that.

We decided I should meet and we should break the news to her mother and stepfather in Nevada over the Thanksgiving holiday. I had since moved to an apartment nearer to work, so I made plans for my parents to meet Doranne. As I expected, my mother welcomed her with warmth and open arms, and I heard no objections from my father (as if it mattered).

Doranne and Nash in the early 1960s

Before we went to Nevada we publicly acknowledged at work that we were a twosome. It was at a company Halloween dance where we appeared in costume, dressed as Romeo and Juliet. Doranne has always been one to appreciate the theatrical.

That Thanksgiving we drove the 300 miles to Henderson. The only advice Doranne heard from her mother was: Remember. Latin men can be jealous.

On November 27, 1955, we stood before the justice of the peace in Las Vegas, Nevada, with her aunt Nellie and husband as witnesses. She was twenty-three, I was twenty-seven. We had known each other for six months. It was for richer or for poorer. In sickness and in health. Till death do us part.

44

In 1953, when I was in the air force in Biloxi, Mississippi, I had no idea that a Southern belle and I would meet in far-off California and get married. Doranne had been born in Tallahassee, Florida, and when I entered the air force in the summer of 1952, she was leaving Florida State University in Tallahassee after two years, returning to Nevada and work.

Her dead father's family had been helping Doranne through college. The women on that side of the family tended to the puritanical and were prone toward becoming churchy schoolteachers, not pretty young sorority girls who would be elected fraternity Dream Girl of the South. The family matriarch, Doranne's father's older stepsister, had decided that Doranne was having too much fun and not being studious enough. When old auntie decided, others abided, so it was go west, young lady.

Doranne's father, Aubert Leland Godwin of Bonifay, Florida, had met Carmen Ada Kendrick, born in Meridian, Mississippi, when she was a coed at Louisiana State University. He had been a young engineer, working for the state road department during the regime of Huey Long. Ada, a warm, affable person, was everything Aubert's womenfolk were not, so it might have been love at first sight.

The newly married couple returned to Godwin country in Tallahassee, where Doranne was born a year later. She was named after her two grandmothers, Dora and Ann. Eight years later, a sister, Judith, was born, named after one of her Godwin aunts.

Aubert Godwin died in 1941 during surgery to correct a diabetic condition. He was thirty-five years old. Mother and daughters lived in Tallahassee although Doranne also spent time with her Grandmother Kendrick in Louisiana. After World War II, Ada married Neal Burt and the family moved to Nevada. Doranne was fourteen years old. It was in Henderson that she attended high school before returning to Tallahassee for two years of college.

Our marriage united three of the oldest strains in North America. Her roots go back to the early English and Irish who settled in the southern United States. On her father's side, the family has been traced to pre-Revolutionary times, and she is eligible to be a member of the Daughters of the American Revolution if she so desired.

The Candelarias go back to the early Spanish settlers in the west during the 1600s, after Don Juan de Oñate had first colonized New Mexico in 1598.

Both of us lay claim to a smidgeon of Native, true American blood. More as a result of family observation than any proof that would satisfy a genealogical society. (Who issued birth certificates back then anyway?) In Doranne's case, her maternal grandfather looked like the head on the buffalo nickel. In my case, a look in the mirror suffices.

The daughter of the American Revolution meets one of Oñate's orphans, while lurking dimly in both backgrounds are the first Americans who greeted both English and Spanish when they came ashore without visas or green cards. In another sense it was like the Mississippi River and the Rio Grande joining to form the Great American Mainstream.

45

My efforts as a writer took a back seat to domesticity for a while. We got appropriately in debt for a little tract house in suburban Orange County. It was among the first of the hordes of tracts that were to spread like blight over what had once been citrus growing country. The grove north of us wafted orange blossom perfume toward this isolated group of houses where young couples were putting in lawns, building redwood fences, installing wall-to-wall carpet, and starting families. It wasn't long before a shopping center replaced the grove, complete with Sears, Roebuck and retail companions.

Our family grew. A year and a half later the first of our two sons was born. Shortly after, Doranne's teenage sister Judy became part of the family, giving us a baby and a teenager at the same time.

I did find a little time to write. Among these early efforts were a couple of science fiction novels, one of which the West Coast editor for McGraw-Hill liked and sent on to the New York office, where it was turned down.

There was also a book about a boy and his stepfather that a couple of New York editors liked and sent encouraging letters about but didn't publish. This was an examination of my trying relationship with my father and the feeling that sometimes the members of our real family are not our blood relations at all but people on our wavelength that we meet on our journey through life. Both Doranne and I acknowledged that we were the oddballs in our respective families. How lucky that we had found each other!

When our son David was between one and two years old, I had my most serious row with my father. It was during one of our weekly visits to my parents in El Monte. That Sunday we went to pick up David, whom my mother had taken for the weekend. Mother was very thoughtful and seemed to sense when Doranne needed a break from child rearing, besides which she and my father doted on their only grandchild.

They had recently come back from a trip to Albuquerque. Visiting the family was always a strain, especially for my father. I could tell when we arrived that he had had a beer or two—it didn't take much. David was sitting in a little red wagon, one of the toys they kept for their grandson's visits.

When my father saw me, his demeanor changed radically. The expression on his face froze in rictus, his eyes grew wild. I understand how someone could think that a person had been possessed by the devil. There was that devil look on his face.

As we had walked up to the yard he had been calmly pulling the wagon. Now he suddenly began to pull it faster and turn it sharply from side to side. It was as if he was hoping for an accident, for David to topple or the wagon to overturn.

I went quickly over and picked David up. I couldn't understand what the hell was going on, but I didn't like it. Then the tirade began. I don't remember all of the details, but it had to do with religion. I no longer went to church. His grandson hadn't been baptized. What did I mean by—. Ridiculous, I thought. I hadn't considered myself a Catholic for almost ten years. My father himself wasn't the best of Catholics. Why the attack?

Then he blurted something about the family, and I could see it. Probably one of his sisters in Albuquerque asked whether or not his grandson had been baptized and had asked in a needling way what kind of a grandfather he was. Didn't he have any control over his own family?

My mother was horrified at the outburst. I had seen her concern when my father was whirling the wagon about. No doubt she had already taken care of saving David's soul by baptizing the child herself. That didn't bother me. That was her business.

I was angry about the careless way my father had been pulling the wagon, as if he wanted to hurt David. This church business just added fuel to the fire, and we exchanged angry words. I suppose the circumstances of my own birth and my subsequent independence were at the root of the problem. In retrospect I always sensed that my paternal aunts had been more than solicitous to me as a boy. Perhaps they worried that this poor little almost-bastard needed special attention so that he would follow the path of the righteous. I had always thought their concern was because I was

David Candelaria in the summer of 1958 (top)
David, February 1959 (bottom)

a sweet kid. Whatever, any such criticism by his sisters must have been a knife-thrust in my father's side, a reminder of youthful . . . what? Passion? Love? The normal human inability to always control oneself? An act that could be viewed by the unforgiving or the malicious as sin. A Catholic sin.

I had no such thoughts at the time. I was just outraged at his behavior and our words escalated unbearably. I put down David and started toward my father, ready to strike him. Luckily my mother stepped between us, chastising him for his outrageous behavior, and dragging him toward the house.

"That's it!" I shouted. "We're going! If you can't behave and act civilized when we're here, we won't come anymore! You're no father of mine!"

I disowned him. I meant it. My mother knew I meant it, too. I had inherited my stubbornness from her. I was slow to anger, but once angered, slow to forgive.

It must have been five or six weeks after that run-in when the telephone rang one evening. "Hello," the voice on the other end of the line said. "This is the old crab." It was my father. It was the closest he could come to an apology.

46

The year 1959 was not a very good one. I was not making progress as a writer although I was still writing; there was always a project under way. I was learning to be the parent of a baby and of a teenager at the same time. I had also taken up the classical guitar with lessons once a week from a teacher whose greatest thrill in life was that he had once carried Andrés Segovia's guitar for him before Segovia went on stage for a concert. I practiced during what free time I had in an already busy schedule. And work was chaotic!

I was not aware of how thin I was spreading myself. The major strain was work; I was still with the analytical instrument company where Doranne and I had met. By this time I had transferred from the technical writing group supervised by my friend Lew Hodgson to the advertising department. I saw more creative challenges and more opportunity there. But the country was in an economic recession. The company had tightened its belt and increased the pressure to squeeze more performance from those employees lucky enough not to be laid off.

It reached a state of crisis one day when the department manager didn't come in. His wife telephoned. He had gone to the doctor for what he thought was indigestion—too much spicy Mexican food for dinner—and collapsed in the doctor's office. It was a bleeding ulcer. They removed part of his stomach. He would be out for weeks.

Business was warfare. We were in the trenches fighting the enemy (our competitors). When the captain fell, someone came forward to lead the troops. I stepped into the breach to do both his job and mine. I found myself moving at a trot from crisis to crisis, from meeting to meeting, instead of at a walk like a reasonable human being. It was as if I was driven by the hands on my watch, which moved forward too quickly. If I couldn't slow them down, I would have to run faster. There was never enough time.

It didn't take long before I felt sharp pains in my gut, and I thought I was working on my own ulcer. It was something I had vowed never to succumb to, not wanting to follow in my father's footsteps, who by the same time in his life had had the first of his stomach operations. After an examination, my family doctor told me there was nothing wrong with my stomach.

I felt as if I was on a merry-go-round. First a stressful, double-paced day at work. Then home to make an attempt at being a husband and father. Rush to practice the guitar. Squeeze time to work on my writing project. Then back to work. The hamster was racing furiously in his circular cage, but never running fast enough.

I was a mess. One day, speeding in traffic, I looked at the concrete pillars along the freeway. It was as if they were hands gently beckoning to me. Just a little turn of the steering wheel and a sudden added pressure on the accelerator. Smash! My problems would be over. That thought scared the hell out of me. I went to a psychiatrist, thinking that perhaps I was losing my mind. Stress, he said. He had other patients who worked for that same company. He prescribed tranquilizers.

I added my own prescription: I needed to change jobs, to stop trying to do too much. The place was a meat grinder. But it didn't make sense to complain about a meat grinder if I stuck one hand into the blade while turning the crank with the other.

It took a year for me to calm down, for the stomach pains to disappear, for the trembling hand to steady. I stopped wearing a wristwatch and tried to free myself from being a slave to time. I practiced letting things slide, settling for less than perfection, and I found that the world didn't collapse. I discovered that no one else noticed the imperfection but me. I learned to say no instead of always obliging. One may kill the father and the guru and the Buddha, but finally one must always deal with the self.

47

In 1964 I was thirty-six years old and still an unpublished writer. I was calm and comfortable in my work as a promotional specialist for a defense contractor in Orange County. Our son David was seven years old and his brother, Alex, was three. In an attempt to expose our sons to some kind of religious training, we attended the Orange County Unitarian Church.

It was a time of political euphoria for the right wing in Orange County. My ultraconservative boss at work had exulted at the assassination of President John Kennedy just the year before. Our next-door neighbor in the city of Santa Ana was a member of a John Birch Society hecklers' group that disrupted meetings of opposing politicians. Senator Barry Goldwater had proclaimed that extremism in the defense of liberty was no vice, and Orange County had more than its share of self-righteous virtue.

The Unitarian Church was a lonely voice in the county during those turbulent times. With a few other religious denominations, we were working to prevent the rescinding of a fair housing law passed the previous year by the state legislature. It was a cause in which I believed passionately. How could we learn to get along if the law—and bigotry—prevented us from becoming neighbors? I remembered too well the attitudes of the neighborhood in which I grew up in Los Angeles. My wife and I did not want that for our sons. I helped as a fundraiser for the church. My wife and I joined with others—white, black, and brown—knocking on doors and handing out leaflets.

It was not to be. The fair housing law was overwhelmingly rescinded with some two-thirds of the voters choosing to overturn it.

Not long after, our fine minister left in discouragement. Our church had its own extremists. A rift developed between those who wanted to make the church a political bastion in enemy territory and those who wanted to focus

Alex and Ignacio

David (left) and Alex (right)

on the religious needs of the congregation. A new minister, a black man, was hired. When he made his first appearance, some of our church extremists were sorely disappointed. He wasn't black enough.

But there were glimmers of hope in the air. That summer we drove to New Mexico for a visit to the land of enchantment and to pay calls on my relatives. It had been a dozen years since I had been there, the last trip when my father and I had gone just before I went into the air force. There must have been an air of consternation, especially on my father's side of the family. I could imagine the cackling among my aunts. Here was the city nephew, the city cousin of their children, with his gringa wife. Well!

It was a whirlwind two weeks. I don't think our three year old slept the entire time we were traveling. Doranne and I were numb and exhausted, but the family visit was wonderful. When we were at my grandmother's house, my aunts were gossiping how their eldest brother, my seventy-four-year-old Uncle Gaspar, had bought a small red Rambler sedan and drove around Los Candelarias like some teenage hot-rodder. When he pulled into the dirt driveway to join us, he beamed because we, too, had a Rambler, though of a different color.

Things in the country had changed since I had last been there—it would soon be suburbia. The differences that had existed between my cousins and me when growing up had diminished. It seemed as if they were becoming more urbanized, more in the mainstream.

The visit that day was the last time I was to see my grandmother, Eutemia, alive. Because I saw her rarely and never learned Spanish very well, I never knew much about her life. Years later, in doing genealogical research, I discovered that in 1888 she had signed a petition to the U.S. surveyor general to resolve claims to the Candelaria property that still had not been settled forty years after the Mexican War. She was nineteen years old and already taking a strong hand in her new husband's affairs. I often wondered what stories she would have told if I had seen her more often and could have understood Spanish better. She never learned English even though she was born in U.S. territory.

I was pleased that she was able to meet our sons, two of her many great-grandchildren. A blind little old lady dressed in black, sitting on a rocking chair in her little adobe house. She passed away in October 1964, two months before her ninety-fifth birthday.

There was enough excitement about the visit to give my aunts something to talk about for weeks to come. They welcomed us lovingly, fed us to excess, and were thrilled to meet my wife. When it came time to leave, one of my aunts hugged Doranne and paid her the highest order of compliment. "You're not like an Anglo," she said. "You're just like one of us."

Doranne

48

The years went quickly. I left the defense industry and worked two years for an advertising agency in Los Angeles as an account executive and copywriter. The agency had acquired the account of the analytical instrument company that I had left in 1959. Not surprisingly, the agency did not have anyone in its employ who knew anything about the business or about analytical chemistry.

Legend has it that the acquisition of the account was consummated on a visit to the L.A. office of the Federal Bureau of Investigation. The executive vice president of the agency had once been in charge of the local FBI office and, as far as I knew, that was his main qualification for being in the advertising business. Other than that, he was a hell of a salesman and had a reputation as an inveterate joiner of organizations catering to local movers and shakers. My exboss, who now headed advertising and public relations for the entire corporation, was somehow impressed.

Luckily, I had not totally burned my bridges when I left the company, although one of their division managers had once asked me if I wanted to come back to work for him, and I had said no thank you. (I could have said, "Are you crazy?" or "In a pig's eye!")

The agency and company were in a quandary. Now the new agency had to perform. The defense company I had been working for was in one of those periodic downturns that hit the business. After six years I was ready to move on to something more stable.

Work at the agency was a variation on all of the crazy things you read and hear about the advertising business. The place was rife with ambitious climbers who were obsessed with owning a sailboat in Newport Harbor and the right kind of foreign-model sports car. My boss, a senior vice president with a penchant for three-martini lunches, fought to protect his turf.

For many, alcohol was a way of life. In our particular part of the agency there was an alcoholic secretary in addition to my boss. The media manager was another heavy boozer. One of our clients always placed his luncheon napkin over his barely touched food while partaking of a liquid diet, martinis topped off by Irish coffee. When it got to be three o'clock in the afternoon, someone from the office would telephone the restaurant: His boss, my ex-boss, was looking for him.

I did not like to drink at lunch and in other ways was not very politic. In my purist, ignorant way, I neglected to take one of the client's marketing managers to lunch often enough. He pressured my boss to fire me off the account. This meant hiring someone else to do lunch while I stayed out of sight, still writing their advertising. The marketing manager's pleased comment was, "You see how much the advertising has improved now that you fired Candelaria?"

The saddest thing was that after I left this Machiavellian merry-go-round my agency boss drove out to the desert, attached a hose to the exhaust of his expensive automobile, and breathed his last. He had been displaced in an agency coup, and it was more than he could bear.

I had been putting in long days, commuting via freeway from suburban Orange County to the office on Wilshire Boulevard in Los Angeles. Our youngest son, Alex, who was then six years old, said to me one day, "Dad, I never see you anymore. When I get up in the morning you're gone to work. When you get home at night I've already gone to bed." It really upset me and brought tears to my eyes. He was right. We either had to move closer to my work, or I had to find another job.

That was what brought us to Silicon Valley in 1967, where I took a position as an advertising manager for a science company. Away from the agency madness, I had more time for my family and, I hoped, for my fiction writing.

49

Life, as one of my scientific cohorts might say, is definitely nonlinear. During all of this time that I was husband and father and therefore of necessity a wage earner, the desire to write was like a candle flickering in the dim recesses of my mind. But flicker it did, with an undying flame. From whence it came I'll never know. It didn't matter. The point is, the tiny flame was there, ready to become a bonfire at the proper time.

I remember the owner of an advertising agency in Southern California who had approached me at least twice over the years about joining his firm. This flirtation was never consummated. He always concluded that I wanted a job that I could do with my left hand while writing a novel with my right. For my part, I thought that he wanted a slave whose every waking moment and thought were dedicated to enriching his business. A business, as he stated self-righteously, that would never accept an account for alcoholic beverages or tobacco. The likelihood of his small agency being offered any such account was as remote as my joining the choir to sing in his church, about which he liked to piously name-drop. Hallelujah, I thought. I believed that I was more right than he—and less of a hypocrite. I always believed in giving full value on my job, but it was never my entire life. And I was not about to be any employer's slave.

On the other hand, neither was I a slave to art. The writer whose work I most admired might say in an interview—whether he believed it or not—that "the 'Ode on a Grecian Urn' is worth any number of old ladies," but it was definitely *not* worth my wife and children. There was more to life than either job or art.

The new wage-earning situation was a vast improvement. It was a ten-minute drive from home compared to the hour-and-a-half commute each way

Nash with his first published novel, Memories of the Alhambra

in Southern California. I went home for lunch most days. I had more time for family and even a little time to revise my seventh attempt at a novel I had started before we moved. As our sons became older, I more and more wanted to impart to them something of their Chicano heritage, and I unconsciously moved toward writing about it.

This book was a predecessor to my first published novel, *Memories of the Alhambra*. *Dandy* was the story of the brother of José Rafa, one of the main characters in *Memories*, only I gave Dandy a different surname—I had not yet conceived of the Rafas. While this downbeat novel was not quite successful, something was happening. With this book I had returned to my New Mexico roots.

Something was happening in real life too. Over the previous decade or so I had made sporadic forays into my family genealogy. Out of curiosity and perhaps for justification. Of what, I was not exactly sure. Perhaps that I truly was as American as anyone else. I had so often heard the plaintive protest from New Mexicans that our ancestors had come here before Plymouth Rock. Before the Pilgrims. As if that would assuage some pain, some sense of exclusion. The cry falling all too often on the ears of people who couldn't care less. So what if we had come first? They were white, and white was right! Or so it seemed to some New Mexicans. Not to speak of the unmentionable, our Native American side, the ancestry that many in my family would not acknowledge or discuss.

But tracing genealogy by writing letters was both slow and not always successful. Even with church, Spanish, and Mexican records going back to the seventeenth century. I never did find all of the connections back to that first Candelaria in the New World. What did result was that over the years I learned more about my ancestry.

One of the most significant and memorable events of my life took place during that period at a football game in Stanford Stadium. I had taken our youngest son, who was then about ten years old. The Stanford University Indians, as they were then known, were playing the University of Washington. The Washington team was quarterbacked by a real American Indian named Sonny Sixkiller. Sixkiller was a marvelous athlete. His right arm was like a bow slinging arrows to his receivers, and he was quick. This real Indian was running circles around the Stanford team.

We were sitting high in the north end of the stadium, looking across the length of the football field. The south end was open, the seats only rising about half as high as in the rest of the stadium. A grove of trees outside filled this notch.

During the third quarter I looked up from the Indian war dance on the field toward the trees. At first I thought my eyes were playing tricks on me. The grove faded and wavered, like a mirage floating in the distance. Then the trees snapped into focus, cleanly and sharply as if viewed from an old-fashioned stereopticon. They stood out from the surroundings with an intensity that was frighteningly otherworldly. It was as if I could see into, through, and around them all at once.

I was filled with a sense of fear and awe. I couldn't believe my eyes. I was oblivious to what was happening on the playing field, although I could hear the dim roar of the crowd off in the far distance. I knew that if I continued to stare at the trees I would faint.

Along with this fear and awe I had the incredible feeling that somehow I myself had faded, had melted into the trees and the stadium, into the crowd and Sonny Sixkiller. I felt myself wavering like the verdant grove. As if some great hand on the universal switch was flicking it on and off, pulsing this incredible experience through me. I was overcome with a sense of oneness with everything in the universe. It was like nothing I had ever experienced before. I waited to hear thunder from the clouds, a voice from the heavens— but there was only the din of the crowd cheering Sonny Sixkiller. I looked away from the trees, wondering if I was having a life-threatening attack, a hallucination leading to a stroke.

Minutes passed as if they were but seconds, as time sometimes passes when you're in a deep state of meditation. I peeked at the trees, not quite believing what had happened. But every time the powerful feeling would overwhelm me, and I would quickly turn away in fear. Finally, the feeling subsided. The last time I looked at the grove the trees faded gently, then snapped back into focus without the intensity of that first time.

The experience was like an earthquake with minor tremors lingering afterwards. Not many days later we were driving along a Northern California freeway through beautiful hillside country. We stopped at one of the vistas along the way, and while I was staring into a grove of trees I had a faint reminder of that first experience. The trees stood out with incredible sharpness, intensely three-dimensional. But this time it did not frighten me. It was like an old friend saying hello.

I was trained as a scientist and as such have always used doubt as one of the lenses through which I view the world and attempt to understand it. Yet there are things beyond explanation that I can only accept. This was one of them. Somehow, I think the universe spoke to me that day. And occasionally sends me a reminder. About the oneness of all, which we often give lip service to but seldom experience. Experiencing it is enough to affect you for a lifetime.

50

I suppose every decade is unique in its needs—and conflicts. Much as we want to be private people and live outside of society's turmoil, outside of history, we are all children of our times and are affected. This is true whether we live in urban centers in California at the forefront of change or on suburban farms or in remote villages in New Mexico. There is always a problem or crisis of the day clamoring for your attention, distracting you from your main mission, which is to live life itself.

Doranne and I were not immune. For a time we belonged to a group that was . . . I'm not really sure. Call it a study group. A movement. New Age. A sect. A cult. Whatever. It began as a study group, an alternative look at Jesus's teachings in a way that was nondenominational and outside the mainstream of orthodox religions that tend toward the literal and the institutional. Its goal was no less than to change the world—by changing ourselves. And to achieve this, it dipped into the psychological with encounter group sessions that were a fad at the time.

The goals were honorable and sincere. But like so many such commitments, it devoured our time, more time than I finally wanted to give since that meant taking it from elsewhere: from family, when my oldest son needed more of me than he was receiving, and from my writing, whose candle flickered dimly.

It was at one such seminar that the leader pointed to a map of the United States and said, "Show me home." Although I was born in Los Angeles, my ancestral home was New Mexico.

Among the other exercises we undertook was to write our obituary. What did we want it to say? How did we want to be remembered? After loving husband and father, I wanted to be remembered for writing about the

Hispanic people of New Mexico and their history. The next logical question was: What was I doing about it?

Of the seven novels I had attempted, trying to teach myself to write well, only two had Chicano backgrounds. My genealogical research was sporadic. As our sons grew older, I more and more wanted to impart to them something of their Hispano-Indian heritage, to deal directly with what my father had avoided all of his life.

Tracing of family genealogy should have been easy. The Candelarias had lived in the same place for almost 300 years. They were Catholics, and the Catholic church kept good records. Old Spanish and Mexican government records were available in Santa Fe, which had been founded in 1610.

But my search had come to a dead end. Church records in Albuquerque, where my family came from, had been sent to Santa Fe and lost. Other records—like land records for periods in the 1820s and 1840s—had also been lost. Apparently there had been a fire of unknown origin and many records had been destroyed.

This gap in information caused me to rethink the project. I really didn't need a neat genealogical tree back to . . . where? I thought. To Europe? To an Indian pueblo in the southwestern United States? To Adam and Eve? In a way I suddenly saw that the project was not necessary. I had a good deal of information about the past. What was *more* important was the present!

Aside from some general knowledge about the Candelarias in the New World, this search and its rethinking did something else. It made me consider something that the genealogical tree would never show: How it must have been for my ancestors to overcome what they had to overcome in order for me to be here now. And for our sons to be here as the new generation. To me this was an overwhelming, mind-boggling consideration. We exist here—this moment—by divine grace. If the long, thin thread that connects each one of us to the very first humans had been snapped anywhere back through tens of thousands of generations, we would not be here today. And how some of those humans in the past struggled and endured and overcame is important and worthy of being remembered.

So I gave up the genealogical search. I had read New Mexico history. I would add to what was known by imagining myself into the past and what it must have been like for those generations of New Mexicans to become Americans.

These strands coalesced one evening while I listened to a classical guitar recording by Andrés Segovia. It was Francisco Tárrega's haunting "Recuerdos de la Alhambra," a tremolo in a minor key. As I listened I was overwhelmed by a painful feeling of nostalgia. For things lost and for things that never were. The idea for a novel came to me in a flash.

It was a chilling, exhilarating experience—like having a visitation from an archangel. The book would be a culmination of much I had gone through myself and much that I saw in my own family and others from New Mexico. It would be about Mexicanness and the acceptance of it. I had finally found my subject.

51

I began writing *Memories of the Alhambra* in 1973. I rose early each morning, meditated, than sat in the quiet and wrote for fifteen, twenty, or thirty minutes before I had breakfast and went to work. I was like a high-pressure boiler, slowly bleeding off steam to keep from blowing apart. It was not only a novel about Mexicanness; it was also what I imagined it must have been like for my parents to leave the New Mexico farm and make their way in Anglo U.S.A.

Memories is a story about one man's search for his origins. The protagonist, José Rafa, rejects his mestizo origins and claims only his Spanish heritage. Yet, because of social attitudes and his own life experiences, he has doubts. Now, at retirement age, he leaves California, where he had moved to from New Mexico, and goes on a journey first to Mexico and then to Spain to verify his Spanish roots.

It would be two years before I finished writing the novel.

During that time I had to go to Switzerland on business. My wife and youngest son joined me, visiting Italy while I worked. Then we flew to Madrid, rented a car, and toured southern Spain.

I combined the vacation with observations and research for the novel I was writing. I was especially anxious to track down a book, *Catalog of Passengers to the Indies During the 16th, 17th, and 18th Centuries,* a reference to which I had found in the Bancroft Library at the University of California, Berkeley. It had been published by the General Archives of the Indies in Seville, but an inquiry by letter had failed to receive a response.

Part of an afternoon in the National Library in Madrid failed to turn up the book. On a visit to a shop specializing in old books I learned that it was out of print. The Archives of the Indies were closed the days that we were in

Alex and Nash

Doranne and David

Seville. My searches in Spain were as much a dead end as my genealogical research in the United States.

In exasperation I wondered why I was doing this research. So what if I traced my heritage back to Adam and Eve? What did it prove? What did it matter? I decided that I would take what information I had and use it in my novel, inventing whatever was missing.

After the novel was published, I received a letter from a professor at the University of Notre Dame. Was there really such a book as *Catalog of Passengers to the Indies During the 16th, 17th, and 18th Centuries*, or was it strictly fiction? I replied, giving him what information I had about its existence. As a result, he applied for a grant and spent a summer in Seville doing research at the archives.

Back in the United States, I continued working on the novel. When I finished it, Gary Wolf, a friend of mine at work and a published science-fiction novelist, asked to read it. Gary became quite excited about the book and wrote to his agent in New York, suggesting that he consider taking it on. After having the manuscript for some weeks, the agent wrote to me. Sorry. He didn't think it was salable. Fiction publishing was in a terrible state in 1975 as the costs of paper and printing soared and the sales of serious fiction declined. Then again, he added, he might be wrong. This particular novel was just not his cup of tea. Perhaps I should try a few publishers on my own.

Gary was more successful. The screen rights to his novel *Who Censored Roger Rabbit?* were sold to the Walt Disney studios and a few years later became the highly acclaimed movie *Who Framed Roger Rabbit?*

As for *Memories*, I contacted publishers on my own. A few were no longer publishing fiction. The others were not interested. Then I read a newspaper item about a local Chicano writer, Ray Barrio, who was teaching a course on how to publish your own book at the local community college. With my advertising background I could have managed on my own, but it never occurred to me, and I took the course to learn what I could.

At the same time I came to a realization: How could I ask an established publisher to invest a certain amount of money in publishing my novel if I did not have enough faith to do the same? Here I was, cursing the short-sightedness of commercial publishers for not doing what I did not have the courage to do myself.

There was another consideration too—one that I was later asked about by other Chicano writers: Were any of the publishing problems I encountered racially founded? I didn't think so—but then, how could you know? What I felt was that many publishers would publish anything that they thought would make money. Just take a look at any newsstand or bookstore, a cross section from the vulgar to the sublime. What I thought was that publishers did not understand Chicano books because they didn't know about the culture. This no doubt created a barrier to seeing any quality or sales potential in Chicano writings. But even back then Latin American writers were published in English translation without prejudice. The real problem with Chicano writings was the same old story: prophets without honor in their own country, and ignorance.

It is easy enough to mistake ignorance for prejudice, for ignorance is one of its root causes. But to shout prejudice at every rebuff can be a mistake, and it can also be a cop-out for not fighting harder to attain your goal.

So I published and then promoted and sold the book. I had never intended to be a publisher, but I felt so strongly about the novel that I had to. And I learned that I was in good company: James Joyce, Anaïs Nin, Mark Twain, Walt Whitman, Virginia Woolf, and countless others had done the same.

I learned two things from that publishing venture. First, that it's probably more work to publish, promote, and sell a book than it is to write it, and writing is more fun. Second, it helped me overcome the flawed thinking that if a commercial publisher did not accept my book, then it was not worth publishing.

The publishing course was two half-day sessions on Saturdays. After one session I spoke with Ray Barrio, whose self-published novel *The Plum Plum Pickers* was about agricultural workers in the Santa Clara Valley of California. We were the only Chicanos in the class, and he asked me if I was a member of the movimiento, the Chicano movement that was the equivalent of the black civil rights movement. I said no. I was, I suppose, in the eyes of the more militant, an assimilated Chicano who did not even speak the language. A member of the detested mainstream. A bourgeois.

When he asked about my book, I told him that it was based on my family, who were from New Mexico. (I had not realized that I had written a Chicano novel.) He told me, in confidence, that there were Chicanos in New Mexico who insisted that they were pure Spanish. Manitos, he called them—short for hermanitos, which meant little brothers.

I told him that *that* was what my book was about: A New Mexican who denies his Mexicanness, claiming to be of pure Spanish ancestry. He was taken aback and quite anxious to read it. Ray later wrote the first review of *Memories of the Alhambra*, a glowing testimony that I used in promoting the novel.

52

There I was in 1977, a self-published first novelist—at the age of forty-nine. It was about time. Oh, to have been twenty-five and discovered, lauded with comments like "sensitive," "perceptive," "shows brilliant promise." At forty-nine the careers of most writers are at their zenith or waning rather than beginning. The only question that came to mind was, what took so long?

Similar to the book's writing, its publishing took two years. I selected the typeface, designed the way the text fit onto the printed pages, and dealt with a typesetter supported in part by a grant from the National Endowment for the Arts. I pasted down the typeset pages, two pages per form, as required by the typical printer. One artist friend designed the book jacket while another did the oil painting illustration that appeared on the jacket. I dealt with a printing broker who placed the job with a midwestern firm that specialized in short runs of books. I remember when the printed books arrived, box after box on pallets placed unceremoniously on the curb in front of our house. Where the hell was I going to store them?

Throughout the publishing process real life went on. The year 1976 was particularly eventful. July 4, 1976, was our country's bicentennial. The company I worked for published a special edition of its weekly newspaper, featuring brief contributions from employees whose ancestry could be traced back to early America.

Of the twenty contributions, four were from employees whose ancestry went back to the early Spanish-Mexican settlers. A company photographer was a descendant of explorer Cabeza de Vaca. One young man had an ancestor who was a troop commander with the expedition that, among other things, founded the Presidio of San Francisco. The family of a woman working on the electronic production line had once owned the rancho that is now the city of Milpitas. And myself, an advertising and promotion manager.

I was struck by the contrast between those past lives with the working folks in high-tech Silicon Valley. The differences were especially notable in the young woman's family history. I realized there was more to explore in my writing than just Mexicanness. There was the why of such things coming about. There was our place in the American scheme of things.

As I wrote the book, I did not think of anything but the writing itself. Now that the book was being produced, I began to realize that somebody might actually read it. Including my parents. My mother, I knew, would take it in stride. She was never one to flinch when looking truth in the face. I didn't know how my father would take it.

I can remember a friend of my sister's listening to her complain about our father when we were young. "That meek little man?" the friend said, unable to suppress her disbelieving laugh. Yes, I thought, public Dr. Jekyll and private Mr. Hyde.

As time passed I recognized more of the Dr. Jekyll in him than of the Mr. Hyde, difficult man though he was. He was a loyal and faithful husband. A good provider who worked hard for his family. Some of my parents' friends told me he had a delightful sense of humor, something I never saw. As I matured I accepted the fact that he was not a demonstrative person who could talk about his feelings, whether good or bad. The emotion I had seen most in him when growing up, anger, receded over the years.

I eventually came to the conclusion so many of us come to about our parents, God love them: They did the best they knew how.

Thus my father and I had reached an accord over the years. I felt that he had mellowed. He no doubt thought that being a settled family man who had given him his only two grandchildren somewhat atoned for my being a heathen. There were still topics of conversation that neither of us could broach. Yet it was a warm relationship in its limited way. We settled for what was possible.

Father had retired from the railway postal service some twelve years previously, had the second of his major operations for stomach ulcers, and recuperated nicely. Bored with retirement, he worked part-time for a bank for a few years before settling down again. He and mother traveled. On one trip to Mexico they were guests at the rancho of a couple they had met on a trip to Spain. The husband had retired as an official in the Mexican postal service in Mexico City. My father and he had become friends and exchanged correspondence from time to time.

As my novel came closer and closer to being a finished product, I became apprehensive about how my father might react to it. He was the prototype for the main character, José Rafa. Some of the incidents in the book were based on real events but were amplified and fictionalized. It dealt with the life problem that I had observed and projected onto my father, a concern that I had to deal with in my own life.

In late July 1976 my mother telephoned. My father was ill and had been hospitalized. It was not stomach ulcers this time, it was more serious—cancer of the pancreas. I flew to West Covina to visit him in the hospital. It was terminal. The only question was whether it would be days or weeks.

I was back home in Northern California a few weeks later when he passed away on August 27, 1976, at the age of seventy-one. Toward the end he had been asking for his son. Doranne, our sons, and I flew down for the funeral. My mother was devastated, but she handled it with typical stoic courage.

Needless to say, my father never read *Memories of the Alhambra*. A year later when my mother read the published book, she looked at me in a strange way as if confronting a shaman and asked, "How did you know all of that?"

53

Memories of the Alhambra made its appearance in April 1977. During the process of publication I established Cibola Press, named after the famed seven cities of ancient Southwest Hispanic lore. My wife was gracious enough to serve as special assistant to the publisher. She used her maiden name, Doranne Godwin, to sign correspondence to reviewers, libraries, colleges, and potential readers.

As both publisher and author, I was able to get a special insight into how that particular book made its way. I received copies of reviews, knew what promotions went out and to whom, and filled each order myself.

Reviews were very positive for the most part. Of the more than two dozen that I saw, only two, both from Spanish-surnamed reviewers, attacked the book. I sensed that *Memories* did not conform to their preconceptions of what a Chicano novel should be, and they trashed it. Among the more vocal advocates of Chicanismo the idea of a Chicano character in a novel rejecting his mestizo heritage and embracing his Spanish roots must have been intolerable. The New Mexico breed, whose story this was, makes up only a small part of the Chicano family, most of whom have more recent origins in Mexico.

A third Spanish-surnamed reviewer, who was highly receptive to the book, hit the nail on the head by seeing it as the story of the dilemma of the New Mexico Hispano. Another Chicano reviewer saw it as a bourgeois Chicano novel, yet seemed to see more than that in it.

The reaction from non-Hispanic-surnamed reviewers was somewhat different. Two in particular were from a western state that has had its share of confrontational Chicano politics. One stated that it went beyond class and racial group. The reviewer said, "We learn that José's pride drove him to detest being called 'Mexican'—he yearned for identification with Spain. For Joe (his son) and Teresa (his wife), it is more important to be called simply a man, a woman, an individual, with no other adjective or proper noun."

The second non-Hispanic reviewer commented, "It is also not a polemic on Chicanos, on the manner in which the Mexican Americans have been held down, discriminated against, and so forth. . . . No waving of Chicano banners here; no paean to the glory of Aztlán. . . . But this book does have a deep, quiet tone of pride in that so-called Chicano heritage. . . . the book also makes clear that the Chicano is a human being, an American whose heritage came from the Iberian peninsula and the American Indians rather than the northern European areas."

Later, when the book had been out for a while, Chicano critics had more to say. The book was described as unsettling and ". . . yet another proof that the Chicano experience encompasses a wide range of possibilities that preclude its being simplistically characterized." One reviewer suggested ". . . we might well expect even more disturbing visions of ourselves from Candelaria's pen." Another reviewer described Theresa as "one of the strongest female characters created so far by a Chicano author."

From another critic, ". . . the novel is a story of a war. It is the grinding war between people produced by the traditions of Hispanic New Mexico, an agricultural, day-to-day, make-do, geographically stable culture, and the materialistic juggernaut of the Anglo-American system." And finally, "The novel does not give answers, but it sets the stage, poses the questions, gives the reader the ability to judge for him- or herself. It is evidence that the Chicano novel has reached a higher stage of development, and also offers evidence that the development will continue."

The nonpolitical novel was in many ways very controversial among Chicano intellectuals, academics for the most part. This self-described Americanized Chicano was criticized by some as being a coconut, brown on the outside and white on the inside. I responded to the Chicano newsletter *Carta Abierta* as follows:

> Becoming a coconut can be one stage in the evolution to "American," whatever that means. I think the big concern is, will these coconuts remember that hard, brown shell on the outside that is part of them? Or will they try to paint that shell white and pass for some other kind of fruit? *Memories* was

written to look at that question and what I think of as the "great American" story—the migrant experience.

The book failed the ethnic/political litmus test for some. It—or rather the author—was not brown enough. But it helped broaden the field for Chicano fiction by breaking through limits of ideological theme and attitudes about identity and ethnicity. It has been described by some as one of the seminal books of Chicano literature. And best of all, in reading to young Chicano college students, I have felt a rapport and tolerance that I did not feel from some of their elders.

54

A year after *Memories* was published I came home from work one day with what I thought was the flu. It did not get better. The mere effort of brushing my teeth was so fatiguing that I had to rest for an hour afterwards. After a few days I went to the doctor. Was it mononucleosis? The hysteria over Legionnaire's Disease was still fresh in mind. The diagnosis was "unknown." It wasn't fatal. It should go away of its own accord.

It didn't go away for four months. In that time I had seen the doctor on several occasions, as much to his exasperation as my own. He finally concluded that there was nothing really wrong with me. It was psychological. I should see a shrink. I knew better. I had no objection to psychiatry, if such was called for. This was something else. I felt acute frustration with that unsympathetic doctor.

A friend told me about a neighbor of his who was suffering from something similar. Then I met a neighbor of ours who was also suffering from the same symptoms. Her husband was a doctor, the boss of the doctor I had been seeing. On my next visit I wielded the club of his boss over my doctor's head, and he sent me on to a specialist. The specialist could take a spinal tap and send it to the Center for Disease Control in Atlanta, but that might be more painful than the disease. It should go away soon.

Slowly I began to feel stronger and started back to work. Two hours a day at first. It was some months before I was at full strength again. Apparently I had been suffering from an early, unrecognized case of what is now called chronic fatigue syndrome.

The four months' illness gave me much time to reflect. I thought of two close friends who had died at age forty, one from radiation-induced leukemia, the other from cancer. I thought of my ex-boss, who had committed suicide, and two other men I had known who had found life more than they could bear in the turbulent 1960s and had done the same.

I also remembered one of the most heartening, positive people I had ever met. I had been on a business trip back East. I was seated on the airplane returning to California when a flight attendant wheeled a passenger down the aisle. The attendant stopped beside me and lifted a young woman who had been strapped into the wheelchair into the seat alongside.

The passenger was obviously pretty helpless. She turned and smiled and in a halting voice introduced herself. We talked during the flight back home. She suffered from cerebral palsy and diabetes. She was living in an apartment by herself with help from someone who came in daily for a few hours.

I told her that I was a writer and promised to send her a copy of my novel. She asked for a piece of paper and pen and laboriously, in large, childlike script, wrote her name and address. She too was a writer, she said, and was working on her autobiography. She had also written a few poems.

Remembering her reminds me of a favorite quotation by William Faulkner, "Between grief and nothing, I'll take grief." But she seemed to have appended to that, "The world is so full of a number of things, I'm sure we should all be happy as kings."

During my illness I became resolved to take time off from work to write full time—for a few years at least. Life was too short. Who knows what might happen. I resolved, too, that I would finish what I envisioned as a trilogy, of which *Memories* was the first book.

The second book would look at the root causes of the sickness from which José Rafa suffered. This I saw as the American conquest of the Southwest, the Mexican War of 1846 to 1848. I would project myself into what New Mexicans of that time must have felt at the aggression of U.S. Manifest Destiny. It was the time when my family, like so many others, became Americans at gunpoint. This eventually became the novel *Not by the Sword*. In it I hoped to counter some of the biased points of view in Willa Cather's novel *Death Comes for the Archbishop*, which reflected conventional American attitudes of the time.

To complete the trilogy, I wanted to write a sequel to *Sword*, titled *Inheritance of Strangers*. This would be set in the time of the coming of the railroad when Hispanic New Mexico was on its way to being Americanized.

Doranne and Nash circa 1982

And it would recount the parallel story of the criminal overwhelming of California, which suffered much more than my native New Mexico during and after the Mexican War. I remembered the young woman on the electronic assembly line whose family had once owned Rancho Milpitas.

The illness had been a sign. I would get well, take pen in hand, mount my own Rocinante, and do battle with the enemy, the White Knight of Ignorance.

EPILOGUE

The second and third novels of the Rafa trilogy were written and published. During the writing I felt the need for a fourth in the series. This was to be a more contemporary novel about contemporary concerns. *Leonor Park* is a story of land and greed in the modern American West. Most of the story takes place during the Roaring Twenties with siblings battling over an inheritance that includes land alongside the Rio Grande. It is set against a background of Chicana flappers and Chicano sheiks, bootleggers, and speakeasies during the transition of a small town to a modern city.

The quartet follows the Rafa family from the nineteenth to the twentieth century with their adaptation to change in a changing world, based on family lore, history, and imagination. As a result of these novels, I have been described as the historical novelist of the Hispanic people of New Mexico.

In addition to the four novels, two collections of short stories have been published, some of the stories first appearing in literary magazines. The stories in *The Day the Cisco Kid Shot John Wayne* and *Uncivil Rights and Other Stories* are contemporary, dealing with the issues Hispanics face as they make their way in an Anglo United States.

The epigraph of *Memories of the Alhambra* is from the T. S. Eliot poem, "Four Quartets":

> We shall not cease from exploration
> And the end of all our exploring
> Will be to arrive where we started
> And know the place for the first time.

Most Americans carry on their lives knowing little about their personal history (i.e., their ancestry). Tracing my ancestral roots to the first known Candelarias in what is now the United States was both a personal and a literary journey. Journey can be self-discovery. To learn truly who you are and what you came from. To accept that and to go forth to do your work in life. History is but one part of it. I see the journey also as a spiritual experience, putting you in touch with the greater truth. And often when your ancestry is denigrated, there is the urge to affirm it by what you learn on such a journey.

Among the things I discovered was the complex of ancestors from which I descended: Spanish, Native American, Mexican Indian, Irish, African. I learned more about myself and developed a deeper appreciation for those who came before. From the Widow Candelaria, survivor of the 1680 Pueblo Revolt in New Mexico, to the unknown Joseph Candelaria who left his mark on Inscription Rock in the New Mexico desert, to Nash Candelaria in the twenty-first century in Santa Fe, this journey has been reflected in my writings about the Hispanic Southwest.

Of course, one does not write for the self alone. Authors ardently hope for readers. For writing is sharing, communing with readers. In this case, it is sharing the stories of an often maligned and ignored culture that is unknown to many, although it has long been an integral part of the great American landscape. Most reviewers have been receptive to the work. Regarding the four Rafa novels, the following are brief examples of a few of their comments:

Memories of the Alhambra was acknowledged as one of the seminal novels of Chicano literature: "More than a brown 'Roots' . . . a story of a people struggling to achieve their ideal of the American Dream" (*Douglas Daily Dispatch*).

Not by the Sword, recipient of the Before Columbus Foundation American Book Award and one of three finalists for the Western Writers of America's Best Western Novel: "*Not by the Sword* addresses a subject that after more than a hundred years of pain is today still taboo: American imperialism, that is, the sense and anguish of Gringo conquest, how our forefathers dealt with subjection, occupation and the spiritual degradation of becoming conquered" (*La Herencia del Norte*).

Inheritance of Strangers, the sequel to *Not by the Sword*: "The subject matter and the grassroots approach is Faulknerian enough, but there the similarity ends. Candelaria's prose is crisp and vivid, flavored with Hispanic distinctness by the patterns and rhythms of the characters' speech. Nor are his characters weighed down by any sense of tragic doom. The feeling that comes through from José Antonio and the Rafas is one of quiet determination to survive and to stay themselves in a world they no longer recognize" (*The Roundup*).

Leonor Park: "With the publication of *Leonor Park*, Nash Candelaria continues to gain stature as an American writer. . . . Candelaria's greatest strength manifests itself in his capacity to draw and motivate characters. Nicolas, Leonor, Antonio Rafa, and a host of minor characters like Magdalena's cook, Lupe, Leonor's cousin, Theresa, and the ne'er-do-well Trujillo brothers are all skillfully portrayed, but in the character of Magdalena Soto Candelaria creates something special, a masterpiece of near diabolical proportions, a woman who is at once despicable and pitiful, and—it must be said—comic, for even as she moves heaven and earth to do her brother in and triumph majestically over all comers, the evil schemes she sets in motion become so absurd that one cannot help but laugh even as one deplores her greed. Taken together, Candelaria's characters comprise a robust whole; considered singly, Magdalena is in a class by herself, and in creating her, Candelaria has given *Leonor Park* a powerful force" (*The Texas Review*).

The short stories express my personal concerns about the present lives of Hispanics in the United States. Some stories, like "The Day the Cisco Kid Shot John Wayne," are based on personal experience. Others are based on observation and imagination. Here, too, the works have been well received by many reviewers.

The Day the Cisco Kid Shot John Wayne: "The twelve stories included in this collection provide an unusually perceptive picture of family relationships, especially the inter-generational and inter-racial misunderstandings which are commonplace between Hispanics and Anglos. Candelaria revealed his sympathetic understanding of these themes in his early novel, *Memories of the Alhambra*, but his short stories are especially successful in their probing of human emotions and vulnerability. There is joy and hope and endurance in his characters, too, and these positive values are often contrasted with loneliness and the fear of death, as in 'Kissing the Gorilla' and 'Affirmative Action'" (*Western American Literature*).

Uncivil Rights and Other Stories, from which the story "The Dancing School" was one of three finalists for the Western Writers of America's Best Western Short Fiction award: "*Uncivil Rights* is a little cultural gem, the kind of literature that you still find enchanting even after a second read. Candelaria's stories and characters exist not just in the author's mind but also in the llanos and the mountain villages of New Mexico. Only a New Mexican would know that a cow can, in fact, get arrested for trespassing on government property even if she cannot read. Candelaria writes with a genuine grasp of la raza and its roots. *Uncivil Rights* is a funny and absolutely candid snapshot of Hispanics in the Southwest" (*El Paso Times*).

At least three of the stories in the two collections have been included in a number of anthologies. The stories "The Day the Cisco Kid Shot John Wayne" and "El Patrón" have been widely anthologized. "Dear Rosita" was included in a collection for middle school students. These anthologies have been general collections, collections about growing up ethnic in America, as well as numerous collections aimed at young people, from middle school through high school to college. The stories have found their way not only to Hispanic students to help them learn about their long-time heritage in the United States, but also to non-Hispanic students who may for the first time be exposed to another group in the great American mosaic of cultures. This has been especially gratifying.

It's not often that writers get direct responses from their readers. With the development and wide availability of the Internet, students and teachers have found their way to this writer with their questions and comments. Though occasionally I can't help but smile when the nature of a student question is such that I suspect the computer-literate young soul in cyber space is really hoping that I can do his homework for him. That aside, requests have been cheerfully answered. Some of them have been detailed questionnaires about particular writings. Two examples are not untypical.

A class at the University of Nebraska submitted a series of questions about *Not by the Sword*, which they were studying, showing an astute perception about the story and a curiosity about the history of the American takeover of New Mexico during the march of Manifest Destiny.

These e-mail requests are not limited to American students. A student at Udine University near Venice, Italy, submitted an interview by e-mail, an extensive series of questions not only about specific writings but also about my own history as well as the history of Hispanics in the Southwest. This for her graduation thesis at the university. What makes it so worthwhile was to have received an e-mail almost two years later that she had received a Fulbright scholarship to teach and study at Mount Holyoke College for women in Massachusetts and that her thesis contributed to her being awarded that scholarship.

There are rewards greater than money. These interactions with students are part of that greater reward.

One of the questions frequently asked (no doubt asked of most writers) is, why did you become a writer? It is a difficult question to answer. The best I can say is that I don't exactly know, that there is just something within me that has to come out.

I believe that everyone has a touch of the artist. It's a God-given gift, and the act of creating art brings you closer to the ultimate Creator. Not everyone is lucky enough to get the chance to fulfill that aspect of him- or herself. I consider myself one of the lucky.

Writing is something I have to do. It gives me great pleasure. I have never suffered from writer's block. When I sit down at my personal computer, the lighted monitor peering at me like a giant eye, and I start to work, time flies, and I often dissolve into a state that approaches meditation. It's as if I am the medium through which the words flow to the computer. When it's going well, I'm not overtly conscious of the words themselves. It's as if my fingers have their own life, transmitting from that source beyond to what appears on the screen.

I wouldn't be happy not writing. And I will continue to write my stories until I no longer have the strength or life to do so.

Excerpts from the works mentioned above can be found online at http://www.asu.edu/brp/Candelaria/excerpts.html.

ADDENDUM

After completing this book, I discovered additional information about my ancestors. These details did not seem appropriate to include in the main body of the memoir but do shed light on the complexity of my family history. Few Americans know much about their ancestors except perhaps vague family lore that may or may not be true: titled ancestors, fortunes lost, association with famous people, acts of bravery, infamous escapades. I was intrigued to learn about Blas de la Candelaria, the first known Candelaria in New Mexico; his widow and the Candelaria matriarch, Ana de Sandoval y Manzanares; and my Irish great-great-grandfather, John Dalton. How had such divergent streams conjoined to eventually produce me, now in the twenty-first century?

Blas de la Candelaria

Little is known of Blas de la Candelaria, except that he died prior to the Pueblo Revolt of 1680. No information was found regarding his parents, his date and place of birth, or his ethnicity. Was he born in New Mexico, Mexico, or Spain? A recent analysis of my DNA showed that the surname Candelaria is of Semitic origin. So Blas or one of his ancestors was a Spanish Jew who may have come to the New World to escape the Spanish Inquisition. Blas was very likely a converso, a Jew who converted to Catholicism under threat of death, and possibly a crypto-Jew, that is, a converso who secretly practiced the old religion.

Ana de Sandoval y Manzanares

A 1675 record indicates that Ana's father was probably Mateo de Sandoval y Manzanares, a mulato libre (free mulatto) native of New Mexico. His wife was Juana de la Cruz, an Indian servant of the miner Capitán Don

Pedro del Pozo, who lived in northern Mexico. At that time in Mexico and New Mexico, Spaniards of higher rank owned African slaves while most mulattos were free.

Mulattos were almost always offspring of Spanish fathers and African mothers. Mulattos whose mothers were Spanish and fathers African were rare. As in most of Latin America there appeared to be no barriers to these matings, in contrast to the English-American colonies across the continent, where importation of African slaves was in full swing. And there appeared to be no barriers to mulattos becoming property owners.

Mateo de Sandoval y Manzanares, very likely the son of a slave and possibly once a slave himself, had become a property owner in New Mexico. The earliest known reference to a Mateo Manzanares, likely the same man, was that in 1636 his estancia (small ranch) was located at some distance from the San Felipe Pueblo, which is between Santa Fe and Albuquerque.

In 1680 the Pueblo Indians, whom the Spanish were trying to convert to Catholicism, grew incensed at their oppression and revolted. The widow Ana de Sandoval y Manzanares was listed as one of the refugees from the Pueblo Revolt, when Spanish colonists were driven from New Mexico into exile near El Paso, Texas, and Juárez, Mexico.

Some 2,500 colonists and their servants survived the massacre and fled the rebellion. Most refugees, including women and children, made the 300-mile journey south on foot.

The best information is that the Widow Candelaria's children were twelve, four, and two years of age at the time of the revolt. One account states that she and her sons packed their few belongings in a carreta and joined the flight. She and the boys rode horses while their servants walked the ten miles to the San Antonio mission church at Isleta Pueblo to join other refugees before escaping south. This particular account does not mention the widow's two-year-old daughter, who presumably rode in the carreta. It seems unlikely that her youngest son could have been much help in packing, either, and also may have ridden in the carreta instead of on horseback.

A 1684 record in Parral, Mexico, indicated that after the Pueblo Revolt, Mateo resettled in Torreón in northern Chihuahua, Mexico, as did numerous other New Mexico settlers. At the same time his daughter Ana was listed in the 1684 El Paso census as the widow of Blas de la Candelaria, living in the village of Corpus Christi de la Ysleta, El Paso, Texas, with her family.

The Diego de Vargas census of the El Paso district of December 22, 1692, to January 2, 1693, recorded Ana and her family in the pueblo of Ysleta as among those loyal to the king of Spain and ready to resettle the province of New Mexico. Her children were Francisco, aged twenty (more likely twenty-four); Feliciano, aged sixteen; and María de la Rosa, fourteen. If Ana was eighteen years old when her oldest child was born, she would have been born in 1650.

Many New Mexicans refused to return in 1693, preferring to remain in Mexico. Those who did return were offered rewards by the government. In all, 70 families, 18 friars, and many Indian allies followed General de Vargas north for resettlement. The Widow Candelaria's household was comprised of 13 people. The refugee caravan included 18 wagons pulled by mules and horses, 3 cannon in carts, 1,000 mules, 2,000 horses, and 900 cattle. While crossing the southern New Mexico desert area known as Dead Man's March, 30 women and children died. The survivors arrived in Santa Fe in mid-December 1693.

Records show that in 1697 Ana and her family were in Santa Fe where they received livestock and supplies from Governor de Vargas: seven and a half yards of lana (wool), six and a quarter yards of bayeta (baize cloth), sixteen mantas (coarse cotton shirting), fifteen sheep, five goats, two cows, and one bull.

On July 13, 1716, Ana returned to the Río Abajo (the lower river area south of Santa Fe), where she claimed land at San Clemente that had belonged to her deceased father and had been abandoned as a result of the revolt. The Widow Candelaria traveled 1,400 miles to Mexico City by burro, staying there almost two years seeking the deed, which was finally granted by Governor Félix Martínez. She had petitioned for the deed in 1716, which means she was at least sixty-six years old when she made that long burro trip south, a hardy woman indeed!

The Manzanares grant, as it was then known, consisted of 110,000 acres (172 square miles) located south of Albuquerque. The property was bounded on the east by the Río del Norte (Rio Grande), on the west by the Río Puerco, on the south by the house of Tome Domínguez (village of Tome), and on the north by a ruin above the pueblo of San Clemente near the present-day Isleta Pueblo.

One of the conditions of the grant was that the owner be able, willing, and properly equipped to work the land. Because of her age, the Widow Candelaria gave the land to her younger son, Félix, who later sold it to Captain Bernabé

Baca. Under the usual practice of inheritance, the land would have gone to her oldest son, Francisco. Why it did not is a mystery. Perhaps Francisco, who was settled on good land in Albuquerque, did not need or want the property. Or perhaps Francisco and his mother were estranged at the time.

It was Francisco who was my progenitor. He and Félix were the heads of families among the founders of the city of Albuquerque in 1706. Perhaps *founded* is too strong a word, though they were among the families who settled the area that was to grow into the modern city. It was one of Francisco's sons, Juan Candelaria, born in 1692, who was the author of an early history of New Mexico, reminiscences recorded in 1776, the year of the Declaration of Independence across the continent.

Ana de Sandoval y Manzanares died in Albuquerque on April 25, 1734, described as muy vieja. She was most likely eighty-four years of age.

John Dalton

The oldest known of my maternal progenitors was my great-great-grandfather, John Dalton. He was born in 1827 in Westmead (Westmeath) County, Ireland, and arrived in the United States as an immigrant, enlisting in the army at Pittsburgh, Pennsylvania, in 1850. This was the period of Ireland's Potato Famine, which prompted many poor farmers to leave the country for a better life in the United States. Many young men joined the army as a means of survival—a job, food, clothing, and shelter.

Dalton was discharged from the army in 1860. He and Emaline Fletcher, his wife of five years, moved to the Santa Fe area of the Territory of New Mexico. He was described as being about five feet eight inches tall, weighing about 140 or 150 pounds, of fair complexion, with dark hair and blue eyes.

On August 30, 1861, he reenlisted in the Union army at Fort Union, New Mexico Territory, with the rank of second lieutenant, taking part in the Battle of Glorieta Pass, where the Texas Confederate army was driven from New Mexico.

After the war he and his family lived in Santa Fe, then later moved to government land on the Pecos River. Dalton Canyon, near Pecos and Glorieta, was no doubt named after him. He and his wife had seven children, six of whom survived.

In 1899 John and his wife moved to Denver, Colorado, but returned to New Mexico Territory intending to take up residence on their land on the

Pecos River. Before they could resettle, he became ill and died. The October 25, 1999, *Santa Fe New Mexican* newspaper reprinted the following from a newspaper article that had appeared 100 years earlier to the day: "Capt. John Dalton is very ill and hopes for his recovery have been given up."

His wife applied to the U.S. government for a widow's pension based on his military service. In it she declares that the only property, real or personal, left by her husband was one wagon that was sold to pay for the funeral and 160 acres of patented government land on the Pecos River. She had tried to sell the land for $300 after her husband's death but had no offers. The land produced no income; originally heavily timbered, its trees had been cut down and converted into lumber. Her husband had no life insurance. She also declared that her children were in very humble circumstances with large families of their own, and they could not afford to assist her. She was destitute. The application was affixed with her mark ("X"). She was obviously a poor woman who could not write and probably could not read. The best information is that Emeline Fletcher Dalton died in 1910 at the age of seventy-four.

It is interesting that my mother referred to John Dalton as Captain Dalton, as did the item in the 1899 *Santa Fe New Mexican*. The National Archives military records show only the rank of second lieutenant. Perhaps he promoted himself, as many did after the Civil War, when "colonels" abounded throughout the South.